Kona Travel Guide 2024

Discover Kona's Natural Beauty, Rich Culture, and Thrilling Adventures: Your Comprehensive Travel Handbook to the Big Island's Hidden Gems and Unforgettable Experiences.

Owen Nelson

Walk with me through Kona!

Copyright © by Owen Nelson, 2024

Table of Contents

Introduction 9
   Welcome to Kona 9
   What to Expect 10
   Purpose of the Guide 11
      How to Use this Guide 11
   Learn About these Interesting Kona Island Hawaii Facts and its share secrets 12
   Why Visit Kona 15
   Travel Tips for Kona 17
      Travel Tips for a First Solo trip 21
Chapter 1: Getting to Kona 24
   Transportation Options in Kona 24
      By Air 24
      By Sea 25
      By Land 25
   Getting Around Kona 25
   Kona International Airport (KOA) - Airport Information 28
Chapter 2: Accommodation Overview in Kona 32
   Recommended Hotels and Resorts in Kona 35
   Recommended Vacation Rentals in Kona 37
      Tips for Vacation Rentals: 38
   Camping Options on the Big Island 39
Chapter 3: Exploring Kona and Nearby Attractions 43
   Must-Visit Attractions in Kona 46
      Kailua-Kona Overview 49
      Coffee Plantations in Kona 52
      Historical Sites in Kona 55
      Beaches in Kona, Hawaii 58
   Outdoor Adventures in Kona, Hawaii 61
   Cultural Experiences in Kona, Hawaii 64
      Hawaiian Traditions in Kona, Hawaii 67
      Art Galleries in Kona, Hawaii 71
Chapter 4: Dining in Kona, Hawaii 75
   Kona's Culinary Scene 75
   Local Hawaiian Cuisine in Kona 78
   Fine Dining in Kona 82
   Casual Eateries in Kona 85
   Vegetarian and Vegan Options in Kona 89
   Nightlife and Bars in Kona 92
Chapter 5: Shopping in Kona 96
   Souvenirs and Gifts in Kona 96

Local Markets in Kona	99
Art and Crafts in Kona	102
Specialty Shops in Kona	106
Chapter 6: Practical Information for Your Trip to Kona	**110**
Tips for a Sustainable Visit to Kona	114
Chapter 7: Planning Your Trip to Kona	**118**
Best Time to Visit Kona	122
Travel Itineraries	124
Itinerary 1: Beach and Relaxation	124
Itinerary 2: Adventure and Exploration	125
Packing Essentials	127
Traveling with Kids	130
Accessibility	133
Useful Hawaiian Phrases	135
Beyond Kona	**138**
Exploring Hawaii Island	138
Day Trips and Excursions	140
Conclusion	**144**
Farewell to Kona	145
Further Resources	145

Kailua-Kona!

A Journey of Aloha: My Unforgettable Adventure in Kona

In the heart of the Pacific Ocean lies the enchanting paradise of Kona, a place where the warmth of the sun matches the warmth of its people. As I stepped off the plane onto the tarmac of Kona International Airport, I could already feel the spirit of 'Aloha' embracing me. Little did I know that this trip would be a journey of discovery, relaxation, and endless adventures.

My days in Kona began with the gentle caress of the morning sun, as I woke up to the soothing sound of waves crashing against the shore. My choice of accommodation, a cozy beachfront bungalow, was the perfect haven for relaxation. The salty breeze from the ocean and the rustling palm trees provided the soundtrack to my mornings, making each day feel like a new beginning.

The first morning, I embarked on a leisurely stroll along the golden sands of Kailua-Kona's shoreline. As the sun painted the sky with hues of pink and orange, I watched surfers catching waves, and locals practicing hula on the beach. It was a glimpse into the vibrant culture that thrived here.

One of my most unforgettable days started with a visit to a local coffee farm nestled in the heart of the Kona Coffee Belt. Surrounded by emerald-green coffee trees, I learned about the meticulous process of cultivating Kona coffee. The aroma of freshly roasted beans wafted through the air, and I savored every sip of that rich, smooth brew, knowing it was a taste unique to this island.

The adventure continued with a hike to the Pu'uhonua o Honaunau National Historical Park. Stepping onto the sacred grounds, I felt a profound sense of reverence for the Hawaiian culture and history. As I explored the ancient temples and royal grounds, I imagined the lives of those who sought refuge in this place of safety centuries ago.

No trip to Kona would be complete without exploring the underwater wonders. Snorkeling at Kealakekua Bay, near the iconic Captain Cook Monument, was a dream come true. Beneath the crystal-clear waters, I swam among vibrant coral reefs and schools of tropical fish. And, to my amazement, a majestic manta ray glided gracefully through the ocean depths during a mesmerizing night snorkel.

As the sun dipped below the horizon, I ventured into Kailua-Kona town for a taste of its vibrant nightlife. From tiki bars to local pubs, the options were endless.

The rhythmic beats of live music and the laughter of fellow travelers filled the air, creating a lively atmosphere that invited everyone to join the fun.

Kona's culinary scene was a delightful surprise. I indulged in fresh seafood at seaside restaurants, savored the flavors of traditional Hawaiian plate lunches, and explored the local farmers' markets for exotic fruits and handmade treats.

One of the most poignant moments of my journey was visiting the Puako Petroglyph Archaeological Preserve. Amidst the ancient lava fields, I traced my fingers over the intricate petroglyphs etched into the rocks by Native Hawaiians centuries ago. It was a powerful reminder of the island's rich history and the enduring spirit of its people.

As my time in Kona drew to a close, I realized that this journey had not only been about exploring a stunning destination but also about connecting with the land and its people. Kona had welcomed me with open arms, and I left with a heart full of 'Aloha'—a love for the island, its culture, and the memories of a truly unforgettable adventure. My trip to Kona had been a voyage of discovery, where every day was a good day, and every moment was a treasure.

Introduction

Welcome to Kona

Kona is a beautiful destination in Hawaii known for its stunning beaches, vibrant culture, and outdoor adventures. Also for **Scuba diving, Coffee, Volcanoe.**

Welcome to Kona! A captivating destination nestled on the western coast of Hawaii's Big Island, also known as the Island of Hawaii. As a travel expert, I'm thrilled to introduce you to this enchanting region, where nature's wonders, rich cultural heritage, and warm hospitality combine to create an unforgettable experience.

Overview of Kona

Kona is renowned for its geographical beauty and unique characteristics. To start, let's delve into a bit more detail:

Location:

Kona is strategically situated on the western shores of the Big Island, offering stunning views of the Pacific Ocean. This location provides a unique opportunity to witness spectacular sunsets over the water.

Climate:

One of Kona's most enticing features is its sunny and consistently pleasant climate.

With an average of over 300 sunny days a year, it's no wonder visitors flock here for an ideal year-round vacation.

What to Expect

Visitor Experience:

When you step foot in Kona, you're embarking on a journey filled with diverse experiences. Here's what you can anticipate:

•   Beautiful Beaches: Kona boasts an array of pristine beaches with crystal-clear waters, perfect for sunbathing, swimming, and water sports.

•   Volcanic Wonders: The volcanic landscapes are truly remarkable. Explore ancient lava fields and witness the power of nature in action at the majestic Mauna Kea volcano.

•   Cultural Richness: Immerse yourself in the rich culture of Hawaii. You can learn about hula dancing, enjoy traditional luaus, and connect with the history of this remarkable place.

•   Kona Coffee: Coffee lovers will appreciate Kona's coffee plantations, where you can taste some of the world's finest coffee right at its source.

Local Hospitality

One of the most endearing qualities of Kona is the warmth and hospitality of its residents. From the moment you arrive, you'll be greeted with aloha spirit, a genuine and heartfelt welcome. Locals are always eager to share their culture, traditions, and insider tips to enhance your visit.

Purpose of the Guide

Guide Overview
Now, let's discuss the purpose of this travel guide:
This guide has been meticulously crafted to ensure you make the most of your Kona adventure. We understand that every traveler is unique, and whether you seek relaxation, exploration, or cultural enrichment, Kona has something special to offer. Our guide is your companion to help you tailor your experience to your preferences.

How to Use this Guide

To navigate through this guide effectively, consider it your roadmap to Kona. Each section will provide valuable insights into accommodations, dining, activities, and practical information. Feel free to explore it at your own pace, selecting the areas that align with your interests and needs.

With this warm welcome and an overview of what Kona has to offer, you're well-prepared to embark on your Kona adventure. Whether you're a first-time visitor or returning to this paradise, Kona's charm will captivate you from the moment you arrive. Enjoy every moment of your journey through this incredible destination!

Learn About these Interesting Kona Island Hawaii Facts and its share secrets

Kona, located on Hawaii Island (often referred to as the Big Island), is a place rich in history, culture, and natural beauty. Here are some interesting facts and lesser-known secrets about Kona and the Big Island of Hawaii:

1. **Unique Climate Zones:** The Big Island is known for its diverse climate zones, ranging from tropical rainforests to arid deserts and even snow-capped peaks on Mauna Kea during winter.

2. **Coffee Paradise:** Kona coffee is renowned worldwide for its exceptional flavor. The Kona Coffee Belt, where the beans are grown, enjoys ideal conditions for coffee cultivation.

3. **Volcanic Birth:** Hawaii Island is the youngest and largest of the Hawaiian Islands. It's still growing due to volcanic activity, with Kilauea being one of the most active volcanoes on Earth.

4. **King Kamehameha I:** Kona is the birthplace of King Kamehameha I, who united the Hawaiian Islands into a single kingdom in the late 18th century.

5. **Petroglyph Fields:** The island is home to ancient petroglyph fields, where you can see rock carvings created by Native Hawaiians centuries ago. The Puako Petroglyph Archaeological Preserve is a notable site.

6. **Green Sand Beach:** The Big Island has one of only four green sand beaches in the world. Papakolea Beach's distinctive color is due to the presence of olivine crystals.

7. **Star Gazing Hub:** Mauna Kea is one of the best places on Earth for stargazing. It's home to several observatories and offers clear skies, high altitude, and minimal light pollution.

8. **Pololu Valley Black Sand Beach:** While many are familiar with black sand beaches, the Big Island's Pololu Valley features a striking black sand beach at the base of towering cliffs.

9. **Hula Origin:** The ancient hula, known as "hula kahiko," has deep roots in Hawaiian culture. Kona played a significant role in preserving and perpetuating this art form.

10. **Kona Historical Society:** This organization in Kona is dedicated to preserving and sharing the history and culture of the area. They host events, exhibits, and historic tours.

11. Night Dive with Manta Rays: Kona is one of the few places in the world where you can go on a night dive or snorkel to see manta rays, which are attracted to the lights used by tour operators.

12. Lava Tubes: Explore lava tubes, such as Thurston Lava Tube in Hawaii Volcanoes National Park, created by ancient lava flows.

13. Captain Cook Monument: The Captain Cook Monument on Kealakekua Bay marks the spot where Captain James Cook, the British explorer, met his tragic end in 1779.

14. Hawaiian Cowboy Culture: The Big Island has a rich cowboy culture, known as "*Paniolo*." Visit Waimea to learn about their history and traditions.

15. Hawaiian Monk Seals: The island's beaches are sometimes visited by Hawaiian monk seals, one of the most endangered marine mammals in the world.

16. Pele's Hair: In volcanic activity, Pele's Hair, fine strands of volcanic glass, can be created and carried by the wind. Be cautious not to touch it as it can be sharp.

These facts and secrets only scratch the surface of what makes Kona and the Big Island of Hawaii so unique and fascinating. Exploring the island and learning more about its history, culture, and natural wonders will undoubtedly reveal even more hidden treasures.

Why Visit Kona

Visiting Kona offers a wealth of compelling reasons that make it an ideal destination for travelers seeking diverse experiences. Here are some detailed explanations of why you should consider visiting Kona:

1. Natural Beauty

Kona is a paradise for nature lovers. The region's stunning landscapes, including picturesque beaches, lush rainforests, and volcanic terrain, provide a breathtaking backdrop for your adventures.Whether you're lounging on pristine shores, hiking through lava fields, or stargazing atop Mauna Kea, Kona's natural beauty will leave you in awe.

2. Sunny Weather

Kona boasts over 300 days of sunshine per year, making it an excellent destination for those seeking warm, consistent weather. Whether you're planning a beach vacation or outdoor activities, you can count on Kona's sunny climate to enhance your experience.

3. Adventure Awaits

For the adventurous traveler, Kona offers a wide array of outdoor activities. Snorkeling, diving, and surfing enthusiasts will find vibrant coral reefs and clear waters teeming with marine life. Hikers can explore trails through lush rainforests or embark on challenging treks around volcanic craters.

4. Rich Hawaiian Culture

Immerse yourself in the rich culture of Hawaii during your visit to Kona. From hula performances and luaus to cultural centers and historical sites, you'll have ample opportunities to connect with the island's heritage. Engaging with locals and participating in traditional Hawaiian customs will deepen your appreciation for the culture.

5. World-Famous Kona Coffee

Kona is synonymous with exceptional coffee. Coffee lovers can tour coffee plantations, witness the coffee-making process, and savor freshly brewed cups of Kona coffee. The unique volcanic soil and climate conditions contribute to the distinctive and delicious flavor of this renowned coffee.

6. Water Adventures

Kona's crystal-clear waters invite you to partake in various water sports and activities. Snorkel with vibrant marine life, dive into underwater caves, or embark on a sunset cruise along the coast. There's a water adventure suited for every level of experience.

7. Volcanic Exploration

The Big Island is home to some of the world's most active volcanoes. Explore the volcanic landscapes, lava fields, and even witness the mesmerizing lava flow if conditions permit. It's an opportunity to witness the Earth's natural forces in action.

8. Relaxation and Serenity

If relaxation is your goal, Kona offers tranquil beaches and serene landscapes. Unwind on the soft sands, enjoy a spa day, or simply bask in the natural beauty that surrounds you. Kona provides the perfect setting for rejuvenation.

9. Warm Aloha Spirit

The people of Kona are known for their hospitality and the *"aloha spirit."* You'll be warmly welcomed by locals who are eager to share their culture and ensure you have a memorable visit.

In summary, Kona's blend of natural beauty, outdoor adventures, cultural richness, and warm hospitality make it a destination worth exploring. Whether you seek relaxation or excitement, Kona has something to offer every traveler, making it a must-visit destination in Hawaii.

Travel Tips for Kona

1. Best Times to Visit

Kona's best weather is typically during the dry season, which runs from October to April. During this period, you can expect sunny skies and pleasant temperatures. If you prefer to avoid crowds, consider visiting in the shoulder seasons (May to September) when the island is less crowded, although there may be occasional rain showers.

2. Currency and Payment
The local currency in Kona, as in the rest of the United States, is the United States Dollar (USD). Most businesses, including hotels, restaurants, and shops, accept major credit cards. ATMs are readily available for cash withdrawal if needed.

3. Respect Local Culture
Hawaii has a rich cultural heritage, and it's important to show respect for local customs and traditions. Here are a few tips:

•   Remove Your Shoes: When entering someone's home or certain businesses, it's customary to remove your shoes. Look for signs indicating this practice.

•   Respect Sacred Sites: Hawaii has sacred places known as "heiau" and other culturally significant sites. Show respect by not disturbing them and adhering to any posted guidelines.

•   Lūʻau Etiquette: If attending a traditional Hawaiian lūʻau, be sure to participate respectfully and follow the lead of the hosts. It's a great opportunity to immerse yourself in Hawaiian culture.

4. Sun Protection
Kona's sunny climate means you'll be exposed to the sun. To protect yourself from sunburn, it's essential to:

• Wear Sunscreen: Use sunscreen with a high SPF rating, and reapply regularly, especially if you're swimming or engaging in water activities.

• Protective Clothing: Consider wearing lightweight, long-sleeved clothing, a wide-brimmed hat, and sunglasses to shield yourself from the sun's rays.

5. Water Safety

While enjoying Kona's waters, keep these safety tips in mind:

• Swim Safely: Pay attention to ocean conditions and heed warning flags. Be cautious of strong currents and high waves, especially during winter months.

• Snorkeling and Diving: If you're new to snorkeling or diving, consider taking a guided tour to ensure safety and explore the best underwater spots.

6. Sustainable Travel

Kona is known for its natural beauty, and it's important to be a responsible traveler. Here's how you can practice sustainable tourism:

• Reduce Plastic Use: Minimize single-use plastics by bringing a reusable water bottle and shopping bag.

• Respect Wildlife: Keep a safe distance from wildlife, including sea turtles and dolphins. Never touch or feed them.

•　　Stay on Marked Trails: When hiking, stick to designated trails to avoid damaging fragile ecosystems.

7. Transportation
Kona offers various transportation options:

•　　Rental Cars: Renting a car is convenient for exploring the island at your own pace.

•　　Public Transportation: The Hele-On Bus system serves the island. Check schedules and routes in advance.

•　　Taxis and Rideshares: These services are available but may be limited compared to larger cities.

8. Local Events
Check for local events, festivals, and cultural performances during your visit. These can provide unique insights into Kona's culture and offer memorable experiences.

9. Emergency Contacts
Keep important contact information handy, including the local police (911), medical facilities, and your country's embassy or consulate if you're traveling internationally.

By following these travel tips, you'll be well-prepared to have a safe, enjoyable, and culturally respectful visit to Kona, ensuring that your trip is filled with memorable moments and positive experiences.

Travel Tips for a First Solo trip

Here's a list of the top 15 travel tips for someone planning their first solo trip to Kona, including advice on transportation, cultural etiquette, and safety:

1. Research Accommodation: Book your accommodation in advance. Kona offers a range of options, from resorts to vacation rentals, so choose one that suits your preferences and budget.

2. Travel Insurance: Consider purchasing travel insurance to cover unexpected events like flight cancellations or medical emergencies.

3. Transportation from Airport: Arrange transportation from Kona International Airport to your accommodation in advance, especially if you're arriving late at night. Options include taxis, airport shuttles, or rental cars.

4. Renting a Car: If you plan to explore beyond Kona, renting a car is advisable. It gives you the flexibility to visit remote areas and beaches.

5. Public Transportation: If you prefer not to rent a car, use the Hele-On Bus system for budget-friendly transportation around the island. Check schedules in advance.

6. Stay Informed About Weather: Be aware of weather conditions, especially if you plan outdoor activities. Kona's weather can vary, so pack accordingly.

7.   Sun Protection: Protect yourself from the strong Hawaiian sun by wearing sunscreen, a wide-brimmed hat, sunglasses, and lightweight, long-sleeved clothing.

8.   Respect Cultural Etiquette: Embrace the local culture by showing respect. Remove your shoes before entering someone's home or certain businesses, and ask for permission before taking photos in culturally significant places.

9.   Learn Some Hawaiian Phrases: While English is widely spoken, learning a few Hawaiian phrases like "aloha" (hello/goodbye) and "mahalo" (thank you) can enhance your experience and show respect for the local culture.

10.   Responsible Wildlife Viewing: If you encounter wildlife, such as sea turtles or dolphins, maintain a safe distance and never touch or feed them. Respect marine life and their habitats.

11.   Ocean Safety: Be cautious when swimming or snorkeling. Pay attention to warning flags and follow lifeguard instructions. It's best to start with calm, protected areas if you're new to ocean activities.

12.   Emergency Contacts: Keep a list of important phone numbers, including local emergency services (911), medical facilities, and your country's embassy or consulate if you're traveling internationally.

13.   Stay Hydrated: The tropical climate can be dehydrating. Carry a reusable water bottle and drink plenty of water, especially if you're active.

14.   Local Events and Culture: Check for local events, festivals, and cultural performances during your stay. These can provide unique insights into Kona's culture.

15.   Solo Safety: While Kona is generally safe for solo travelers, exercise common sense precautions. Avoid walking alone in poorly lit areas at night and keep your belongings secure.

By following these travel tips, you'll be well-prepared to have a memorable and safe solo adventure in Kona, immersing yourself in its natural beauty and rich culture while respecting local customs and staying vigilant for your well-being.

Chapter 1: Getting to Kona

Getting to Kona, Hawaii, is an essential part of planning your trip. Here's a detailed guide on how to get to Kona:

Transportation Options in Kona

By Air

1. Kona International Airport (KOA)

• Main Airport: Kona is served by Kona International Airport (KOA), also known as Keāhole Airport. It's the primary gateway to the region and the most convenient option for travelers heading to Kona.

• Direct Flights: KOA offers direct flights from several major cities in the United States, including Los Angeles, San Francisco, Seattle, and more. These flights are usually the quickest and most straightforward way to reach Kona.

• International Travelers: If you're traveling from outside the United States, you'll likely connect through a major U.S. airport before reaching Kona.

• Rental Cars: Rental car agencies are available at the airport, making it easy to pick up your vehicle and start exploring Kona and the rest of the Big Island.

By Sea

2. Cruise Ships

• Cruise Ports: Kona occasionally welcomes cruise ships, offering passengers the chance to experience the beauty of the Big Island from the sea. Check with your cruise line for specific itineraries and schedules.

• Shuttle Services: If you arrive in Kona via a cruise ship, there are shuttle services and excursions available to take you to various attractions and activities on the island.

By Land

3. Island-Hopping from Other Hawaiian Islands

• Inter-Island Flights: If you're already in Hawaii and want to visit Kona from another Hawaiian island, you can take inter-island flights. Several airlines operate these short flights, connecting Kona with airports on Oahu, Maui, and more.

• Ferry Service: While there is no direct ferry service to Kona, you can explore the option of taking ferries from other Hawaiian islands to nearby ports, such as Hilo on the Big Island. From there, you can drive to Kona.

Getting Around Kona

Once you arrive in Kona, you'll need transportation to explore the region. Here are some options:

1. Rental Cars

•   Convenience: Renting a car is the most convenient way to explore Kona and the entire Big Island. It offers flexibility and allows you to visit remote areas and beaches with ease.

•   Rental Agencies: Several major car rental companies have offices at Kona International Airport (KOA) and in the town of Kailua-Kona. You can pick up your vehicle upon arrival.

2. Public Transportation

•   Hele-On Bus: The Hele-On Bus system serves the entire Big Island, including Kona. It's a cost-effective option for getting around, but be sure to check schedules and routes in advance, as they may vary.

3. Taxis and Rideshares

•   Taxis: Taxis are available in Kona, but they may be limited compared to larger cities. You can hail a taxi or call for one using local taxi services.

•   Rideshare Apps: Uber and Lyft operate in Kona, providing another convenient option for getting around the area.

4. Walking and Biking

•   Walkable Areas: Kona's town center is relatively compact and walkable. You can explore shops, restaurants, and attractions on foot.

•   Bike Rentals: There are bike rental shops in Kona, allowing you to explore locally on two wheels. Biking is a great way to enjoy the coastal scenery.

5. Tours and Shuttles

•   Guided Tours: Consider joining guided tours for specific activities or excursions. Tour operators often provide transportation, making it convenient for travelers.

•   Shuttle Services: Some companies offer shuttle services for airport transfers and tours to various attractions on the Big Island, including Kona. This can be a hassle-free way to explore.

6. Inter-Island Flights

•   Inter-Island Travel: If you plan to explore other Hawaiian islands during your trip, you can book inter-island flights from Kona International Airport (KOA) to destinations like Oahu, Maui, or Kauai.

7. Ferries (for Nearby Ports)

•   Ferry Services: While there is no direct ferry service to Kona, you can explore the option of taking ferries from other Hawaiian islands to nearby ports, such as Hilo on the Big Island. From there, you can drive to Kona.

When choosing transportation options in Kona, consider your itinerary, the places you plan to visit, and your budget.

Renting a car is often recommended for maximum flexibility, but other options are available for those who prefer not to drive. Be sure to plan your transportation in advance to make the most of your time exploring Kona and the Big Island.

Remember to check current travel advisories, flight schedules, and transportation options when planning your trip to Kona, as they can change over time. Safe travels!

Kona International Airport (KOA) - Airport Information

Location:
• Kona International Airport (KOA) is located on the western coast of Hawaii's Big Island, approximately 7 miles (11 kilometers) northwest of the town of Kailua-Kona.

Airport Facilities:
• Terminals: KOA has one main terminal building that serves both domestic and international flights. The airport is relatively small and easy to navigate.
• Airlines: The airport is served by various airlines, including major carriers that offer direct flights to and from the U.S. mainland and other Hawaiian islands.

- Transportation: Rental car agencies, taxis, and shuttle services are available at the airport for your convenience. You can easily rent a car or arrange transportation to your accommodations upon arrival.
- Airport Services: KOA offers essential services such as baggage claim, ticket counters, restrooms, and dining options. There's also a shopping area for souvenirs and last-minute essentials.
- Parking: The airport provides short-term and long-term parking options. Be sure to check parking rates and availability, especially during peak travel seasons.

Getting to and from KOA:

- Airport Shuttles: Many hotels in the Kona area offer airport shuttle services to transport guests to and from the airport. Check with your accommodation to see if this service is available.
- Taxis and Rideshares: Taxis and rideshare services like Uber and Lyft operate at the airport. You can easily request a ride to your destination.
- Rental Cars: Several major car rental agencies have offices at KOA. Renting a car is a popular choice for travelers who want to explore the island independently.

International Travel:
- If you're traveling internationally to Kona, you'll go through customs and immigration at a designated area within the airport. Be prepared to present your passport, visa (if required), and customs declaration forms.
- Kona International Airport has limited international flights, with most international travelers connecting through major U.S. airports like Los Angeles or Honolulu before arriving in Kona.

Airport Code:
- The three-letter airport code for Kona International Airport is KOA.

Flight Information:
- Be sure to check your flight status, gate information, and baggage claim details before your departure. You can find this information on the airport's website or through your airline.

Services and Amenities:
- While KOA is a smaller airport, it provides essential services such as restrooms, dining options, and shops where you can purchase Hawaiian souvenirs and gifts.

Accessibility:
• The airport is accessible to travelers with disabilities, with features like accessible restrooms, elevators, and assistance services available upon request.

Kona International Airport serves as the main entry point for travelers visiting Kona and the western side of the Big Island. Whether you're arriving for a leisurely vacation or a business trip, the airport's facilities and transportation options make it easy to start your journey in this beautiful part of Hawaii.

Chapter 2: Accommodation Overview in Kona

Finding the right accommodation is crucial for a successful trip to Kona. Here's a breakdown of accommodation options in Kona, Hawaii:

1. Hotels and Resorts

• Luxury Resorts: Kona offers a selection of upscale resorts with oceanfront locations, lavish amenities, and stunning views. These resorts often include restaurants, spas, and recreational facilities.

• Mid-Range Hotels: There are several mid-range hotels in Kona that provide comfortable accommodations, convenient locations, and a range of amenities, making them suitable for families and couples.

• Boutique Hotels: If you're looking for a unique and intimate experience, consider staying at one of Kona's boutique hotels. These smaller properties offer personalized service and often reflect the local culture.

2. Vacation Rentals

• Condos and Apartments: Many visitors to Kona opt for vacation rentals, such as condos and apartments. These offer more space, kitchens, and the flexibility to cook your meals. You can find them both in town and along the coast.

•   Vacation Homes: For larger groups or those seeking extra privacy, vacation homes are available for rent. They come in various sizes and styles, from beachfront villas to secluded mountain retreats.

3. Bed and Breakfasts (B&Bs)
•   Charming B&Bs: Kona has charming bed and breakfasts, often run by welcoming hosts. Staying at a B&B allows you to enjoy a more personalized experience and often includes homemade breakfast.

4. Hostels and Budget Accommodations
•   Hostels: For budget-conscious travelers and backpackers, there are a few hostels in Kona offering dormitory-style or private rooms. These are a cost-effective option for solo travelers or those on a tight budget.

5. Camping
•   Camping: If you're an outdoor enthusiast, you can explore camping options on the Big Island. There are campgrounds near Kona and in other scenic locations across the island, offering a unique way to experience Hawaii's natural beauty.

Booking Tips
- Book in Advance: Especially during the peak tourist seasons (December to April), it's advisable to book your accommodation well in advance to secure your preferred options.
- Consider Location: Think about what part of Kona you'd like to stay in. Do you prefer a beachfront location, being closer to downtown Kailua-Kona, or a more secluded setting in the surrounding areas?
- Amenities: Check the amenities offered by your chosen accommodation. Some include extras like free breakfast, Wi-Fi, parking, or access to water sports equipment.
- Reviews and Ratings: Read reviews from previous guests to get insights into the quality and service of the accommodation you're considering.
- Minimum Stay Requirements: Some vacation rentals may have minimum stay requirements, especially during peak seasons. Be sure to check for any such restrictions.
- Cancellation Policies: Understand the cancellation policies of your chosen accommodation in case your plans change.

Kona offers a wide range of accommodation options to suit various preferences and budgets. Whether you're seeking luxury, cozy charm, or budget-friendly choices, you're sure to find the perfect place to stay during your visit to this beautiful part of Hawaii.

Recommended Hotels and Resorts in Kona

Luxury Resorts:

1. Four Seasons Resort Hualalai

• Location: This upscale resort is located north of Kailua-Kona and offers a luxurious beachfront experience.

• Highlights: Enjoy world-class amenities, multiple pools, a Jack Nicklaus-designed golf course, a spa, and exceptional dining options.

• Notable Feature: The resort has a King's Pond, a unique snorkeling pool with over 4,000 tropical fish.

2. Mauna Lani, Auberge Resorts Collection

• Location: Situated on the Kohala Coast, this resort offers a peaceful, secluded setting.

• Highlights: Relax at the spa, play golf on the Francis H. I'i Brown North and South Courses, and dine at upscale restaurants.

• Notable Feature: The resort features a sea turtle conservation program and a black sand beach.

Mid-Range Hotels:
3. Courtyard by Marriott King Kamehameha's Kona Beach Hotel

• Location: This hotel is located in the heart of Kailua-Kona, offering easy access to shops, restaurants, and historical sites.

• Highlights: Enjoy oceanfront views, a private beach, an oceanfront luau, and proximity to cultural attractions.

• Notable Feature: The hotel hosts the annual Ironman World Championship, making it a great choice for sports enthusiasts.

4. Royal Kona Resort

• Location: Centrally located in Kailua-Kona, this hotel is within walking distance of shops, dining, and the Kailua Bay.

• Highlights: Relax by the oceanfront pool, sip drinks at Don's Mai Tai Bar, and enjoy the scenic Kona coast.

• Notable Feature: The hotel hosts the Voyagers of the Pacific Luau, a cultural experience with hula, music, and a buffet.

Boutique Hotels:
5. Holualoa Inn

• Location: Nestled in the charming village of Holualoa, this inn offers a serene, hillside setting.

• Highlights: Experience personalized service, lush gardens, and stunning panoramic views.

•	Notable Feature: The inn is known for its coffee plantation, and guests can learn about coffee production during their stay.

These are just a few of the excellent hotel and resort options in Kona. Depending on your preferences, whether you're looking for luxury, mid-range comfort, or a unique boutique experience, you'll find the perfect place to stay in this beautiful part of Hawaii. Be sure to check availability and book in advance, especially during peak travel seasons.

Recommended Vacation Rentals in Kona

Condos and Apartments:

1. Kona Alii Oceanfront

•	Location: This oceanfront condo complex is in the heart of Kailua-Kona, offering easy access to shops, dining, and the waterfront.

•	Highlights: Enjoy ocean views, a private lanai, a pool, and a BBQ area. The condo units are well-equipped with modern amenities.

2. Kanaloa at Kona by Outrigger

•	Location: Situated on the Keauhou Bay, this condo complex provides a peaceful setting and is just a short drive from Kailua-Kona.

• Highlights: The property features multiple pools, tennis courts, and spacious condos with full kitchens. It's ideal for families and couples.

Vacation Homes:
3. Kona Bay Estates
• Location: This gated community is located right on the coast of Kailua-Kona, offering exclusive access to the ocean.

• Highlights: Stay in luxurious vacation homes with private pools, oceanfront lanais, and stunning sunset views. These homes are perfect for groups and larger families.

4. Kealakekua Bay Bali Cottage
• Location: This charming cottage is nestled near Kealakekua Bay, a renowned snorkeling spot, and is surrounded by lush gardens.

• Highlights: Experience a unique Balinese-style cottage with open-air living areas, a hot tub, and proximity to hiking trails and the bay.

Tips for Vacation Rentals:

• Book Early: Popular vacation rentals tend to get booked quickly, so make your reservations well in advance, especially during peak seasons.

• Check Amenities: Ensure that the vacation rental you choose has the amenities you desire, such as a kitchen, Wi-Fi, laundry facilities, and outdoor spaces.

• Read Reviews: Read reviews from previous guests to gain insights into the quality of the vacation rental and the host's responsiveness.

• Communicate with Hosts: Don't hesitate to communicate with the rental hosts or owners to ask questions and clarify any concerns before booking.

These recommended vacation rentals in Kona offer a range of options, from oceanfront condos to charming cottages and spacious homes. Depending on your group size and preferences, you'll find a comfortable and convenient place to stay while enjoying the beauty of the Big Island of Hawaii.

Camping Options on the Big Island

Camping is a fantastic way to experience the natural beauty of the Big Island, and there are several campgrounds near Kona and across the island. Here are some camping options with recommendations:

1. Hawaii Volcanoes National Park

• Location: This national park offers two campgrounds: Namakanipaio and Kulanaokuaiki. It's a bit of a drive from Kona, but well worth it for the unique experience.

• Highlights: Camp near active volcanoes and explore hiking trails, lava tubes, and the otherworldly landscapes of the park.

• Recommendation: If you're interested in volcanoes, consider camping at Namakanipaio for a chance to witness the park's volcanic activity.

2. Kalopa State Recreation Area

• Location: Situated on the Hamakua Coast, this campground is approximately a 2.5-hour drive from Kona.

• Highlights: Camp in a lush rainforest setting and enjoy hiking through the nearby eucalyptus groves and gardens.

• Recommendation: For a peaceful rainforest experience, consider camping at Kalopa State Recreation Area.

3. Spencer Beach Park

• Location: Located on the Kohala Coast, this beachfront campground is about an hour's drive from Kona.

• Highlights: Camp next to a beautiful white sand beach, enjoy swimming, snorkeling, and picnicking.

• Recommendation: For a beach camping experience, Spencer Beach Park is a great choice.

4. Ho'okena Beach Park

• Location: This beach park is located south of Kona, approximately a 45-minute drive away.

• Highlights: Camp near a black sand beach, swim, snorkel, and potentially see dolphins offshore.

• Recommendation: If you're looking for a relaxed coastal camping experience, Ho'okena Beach Park is a lovely option.

5. Polihale State Park

• Location: This remote campground is located on the western side of the island, about a 4-hour drive from Kona.

• Highlights: Camp on a vast, remote beach with stunning sunset views and explore the rugged landscapes of the Na Pali Coast.

• Recommendation: For an off-the-beaten-path adventure, consider camping at Polihale State Park, but be prepared for a longer drive.

Camping Tips:

• Permits: Check if permits are required for camping, and make reservations if necessary.

• Gear: Bring your camping gear, including a tent, sleeping bag, and cooking equipment.

• Food: Plan your meals and bring food and water, as some campgrounds may have limited facilities.

• Safety: Be aware of wildlife, weather conditions, and ocean safety. Follow Leave No Trace principles.

• Respect: Respect local rules and regulations, and clean up after yourself.

Camping on the Big Island offers a unique way to connect with nature and experience the island's diverse landscapes. Choose a campground that aligns with your interests, whether it's volcano exploration, rainforest immersion, beach relaxation, or remote adventure.

Chapter 3: Exploring Kona and Nearby Attractions

Exploring Kona and the surrounding areas offers a wide range of activities and attractions to discover. Here's a list of things to do and places to explore while in Kona, Hawaii:

1. Kailua-Kona Town:
•	Historic Sites: Stroll through the historic district and visit landmarks like Hulihe'e Palace and Mokuaikaua Church.
•	Shopping: Explore shops and boutiques for souvenirs, Hawaiian crafts, and local art.
•	Dining: Enjoy fresh seafood and local cuisine at waterfront restaurants.

2. Kona Coffee Farms:
•	Coffee Tours: Visit Kona's famous coffee farms, such as Greenwell Farms or Kona Coffee Living History Farm, for tours and tastings.

3. Beaches:
•	Magic Sands Beach: Swim and bodyboard at this popular beach, also known as La'aloa Beach Park.
•	Kua Bay: Sunbathe and snorkel in the crystal-clear waters of this stunning beach.

4. Snorkeling and Scuba Diving:
• Kealakekua Bay: Snorkel in this marine sanctuary and explore Captain Cook's Monument.
• Two Step: Discover colorful marine life at this popular snorkeling spot near Pu'uhonua o Honaunau National Historical Park.

5. Water Adventures:
• Whale Watching: Take a seasonal whale-watching tour (typically December to April) to spot humpback whales.
• Stand-Up Paddleboarding (SUP): Paddleboard in calm bays or rivers.

6. Historical Sites:
• Pu'uhonua o Honaunau National Historical Park: Explore ancient Hawaiian temples and cultural sites.
• Kealakekua Bay State Historical Park: Learn about Hawaiian history and enjoy scenic views.

7. Adventure Activities:
• Hiking: Take hikes in the surrounding hills or visit Hawaii Volcanoes National Park for volcanic trails.
• Ziplining: Experience exhilarating zipline adventures in the lush Hawaiian landscape.

8. Sunset Cruises:

- Catamaran Cruises: Enjoy a sunset cruise along the Kona coast with opportunities for snorkeling and dolphin watching.

9. Luaus:

- Traditional Luaus: Attend a Hawaiian luau to experience traditional music, dance, and cuisine.

10. Stargazing:

- Mauna Kea Summit: Join a stargazing tour at the Mauna Kea summit, known for its exceptional astronomical observatories.

11. Island-Hopping:

- Hilo: Take a day trip to Hilo on the eastern side of the Big Island to explore waterfalls, botanical gardens, and the lush Hamakua Coast.

12. Local Cuisine:

- Try Hawaiian Cuisine: Savor local dishes like poke (raw fish salad), loco moco (rice, hamburger patty, egg, and gravy), and shave ice.

13. Farmers' Markets:

- Kona Farmers' Market: Visit the market in Kailua-Kona for fresh produce, crafts, and delicious snacks.

14. Waterfalls:
- Akaka Falls State Park: Take a scenic drive to see the towering Akaka Falls and lush rainforest.

15. Mauna Kea Visitor Information Station:
- Scenic Drive: Drive up to the Mauna Kea Visitor Information Station for panoramic views and an educational experience about the summit's observatories.

Remember to check for any park hours, permits, and safety guidelines when visiting attractions and engaging in outdoor activities. Exploring Kona offers a blend of Hawaiian culture, natural beauty, and adventure, making it a memorable destination for travelers.

Must-Visit Attractions in Kona

Kona, Hawaii, offers a variety of must-visit attractions that showcase the natural beauty, culture, and history of the Big Island. Here are some top attractions to include in your Kona itinerary:

1. Pu'uhonua o Honaunau National Historical Park:
- Explore this sacred site, also known as the Place of Refuge, to learn about ancient Hawaiian culture, see reconstructed temples, and enjoy snorkeling in the clear waters.

2. Kealakekua Bay:

- Snorkel or kayak in the crystal-clear waters of this marine sanctuary, and visit the Captain Cook Monument, a historical site accessible by boat or hiking.

3. Hulihe'e Palace:

- Tour this historic palace in Kailua-Kona, showcasing Hawaiian artifacts and history, with beautiful oceanfront gardens.

4. Kona Coffee Farms:

- Take a coffee farm tour to learn about the famous Kona coffee and enjoy tastings at local coffee plantations.

5. Hawaii Volcanoes National Park (a bit of a drive from Kona):

- Witness the power of active volcanoes, explore lava tubes, and hike scenic trails. Be sure to check volcanic activity and safety conditions.

6. Mauna Kea Summit:

- Drive to the summit for breathtaking stargazing opportunities and panoramic views of the island. Join an organized stargazing tour for the best experience.

7. Kahaluu Beach Park:
•   Enjoy excellent snorkeling in a protected bay, where you can spot colorful marine life and turtles.

8. Akaka Falls State Park (a bit of a drive from Kona):
•   Discover the stunning Akaka Falls and hike through lush rainforest trails.

9. Kua Bay:
•   Relax on the sandy shores of this picturesque beach with clear waters and great swimming.

10. Puako Petroglyph Archaeological Preserve:
•   Explore this site to see ancient Hawaiian petroglyphs etched into lava rock.

11. Keauhou Bay:
•   Take a sunset cruise or snorkeling tour departing from Keauhou Bay to experience marine life and coastal views.

12. Kaloko-Honokohau National Historical Park:
•   Discover Hawaiian fishponds, petroglyphs, and historic sites in a beautiful coastal setting.

13. Mauna Lani Beach:
•   Relax on the sandy beach, go snorkeling, or explore the nearby Mauna Lani resort area.

14. Whale Watching (seasonal, typically December to April):

- Join a whale-watching tour to observe humpback whales as they migrate through Hawaiian waters.

15. Luaus:

- Experience a traditional Hawaiian luau for a taste of local culture, music, hula, and delicious cuisine.

16. Mokuaikaua Church:

- Visit Hawaii's oldest Christian church, located in Kailua-Kona, and learn about its history.

These must-visit attractions offer a diverse range of experiences, from cultural heritage sites to outdoor adventures and natural wonders. Make sure to plan your visit and check for any entry fees, hours of operation, and safety guidelines when exploring these attractions in Kona.

Kailua-Kona Overview

Kailua-Kona, often referred to simply as Kona, is a vibrant town on the western coast of the Big Island of Hawaii. It serves as a popular hub for tourists exploring this part of the island. Here's an overview of Kailua-Kona and what you can expect to find there:

Location:

• Location: Kailua-Kona is situated on the leeward (west) side of the Big Island of Hawaii, making it one of the sunniest and driest areas on the island.

• Accessibility: The town is easily accessible from Kona International Airport (KOA), which is approximately a 15-20 minute drive away.

Attractions and Activities:

• Historic Sites: Kailua-Kona is home to several historic sites, including Hulihe'e Palace, Mokuaikaua Church, and Kamakahonu National Historic Landmark.

• Shopping: Ali'i Drive, the main street along the waterfront, is lined with shops, boutiques, and galleries where you can find everything from local art to souvenirs.

• Dining: Kailua-Kona offers a wide range of dining options, from casual eateries serving Hawaiian plate lunches to upscale oceanfront restaurants with fresh seafood.

• Waterfront: The waterfront area is a hub of activity, with scenic beaches, a seawall perfect for sunset strolls, and various water-based activities like snorkeling, stand-up paddleboarding, and fishing.

• Kona Coffee: Don't miss the opportunity to taste Kona coffee, which is famous worldwide. You can visit coffee farms for tours and tastings.

Outdoor Adventures:

- Snorkeling: Kailua-Kona is surrounded by excellent snorkeling spots, including Kahaluu Beach Park and Kealakekua Bay.
- Whale Watching (seasonal): From December to April, you can join whale-watching tours to observe humpback whales in the waters off Kona.
- Fishing: Kona is known for its deep-sea fishing, particularly for marlin. Many fishing charters depart from the Kailua-Kona harbor.
- Hiking: There are hiking trails in the nearby hills and even opportunities for more challenging hikes in the surrounding volcanic landscapes.

Events:

- Ironman World Championship: Kailua-Kona hosts the annual Ironman World Championship, one of the most prestigious triathlon events in the world.
- Cultural Festivals: Throughout the year, you can enjoy various cultural events and festivals that celebrate Hawaiian heritage and traditions.

Accommodations:

- Kailua-Kona offers a range of accommodations, including hotels, resorts, vacation rentals, and bed and breakfasts.

Weather:

• Kailua-Kona enjoys a sunny and warm climate year-round, with average temperatures in the 80s°F (27-32°C). It's known for its "Kona coffee belt," where coffee is grown due to the favorable climate.

Kailua-Kona is a charming and lively town that combines Hawaiian history, culture, and outdoor adventure. Whether you're interested in exploring historical sites, relaxing on beautiful beaches, or enjoying water-based activities, Kailua-Kona has something to offer every type of traveler.

Coffee Plantations in Kona

Kona is renowned for its world-class coffee, and visiting coffee plantations is a must for coffee enthusiasts. Here are some coffee plantations in the Kona region where you can learn about the coffee-making process and enjoy tastings:

1. Greenwell Farms:

• Location: Located in Kealakekua, just south of Kailua-Kona, Greenwell Farms offers guided coffee farm tours.

• Highlights: Tour the lush coffee fields, see the coffee bean drying and roasting process, and taste various Kona coffee varieties.

• Additional Info: They have a visitor center with a gift shop where you can purchase freshly roasted coffee beans to take home.

2. Kona Coffee Living History Farm:

• Location: Situated in Captain Cook, this is a living history farm that provides an authentic experience of life on a coffee farm in the early 20th century.

• Highlights: Explore the farm, interact with costumed interpreters, and learn about the history and traditional methods of coffee farming.

• Additional Info: Tours are educational and offer insights into the cultural heritage of Kona coffee.

3. Holualoa Kona Coffee Company:

• Location: Located in the artsy town of Holualoa, this coffee plantation offers tours and tastings.

• Highlights: Take a guided tour of the coffee fields and processing facilities, and savor freshly brewed coffee on the scenic lanai.

• Additional Info: The plantation often hosts art events and features local art in its coffee shop.

4. UCC Hawaii Kona Coffee Estate:

• Location: This coffee estate is in Holualoa and is affiliated with Ueshima Coffee Company (UCC), one of Japan's leading coffee companies.

•   Highlights: Join a guided tour to learn about the coffee cultivation process and taste UCC's Kona coffee.

•   Additional Info: The estate offers a relaxing setting with beautiful views and a cafe for enjoying coffee and light bites.

5. Mountain Thunder Coffee Plantation:

•   Location: Situated in Kailua-Kona, Mountain Thunder Coffee Plantation offers tours of their organic coffee farm.

•   Highlights: Experience the entire coffee-making process, from farm to cup, and sample their freshly roasted beans.

•   Additional Info: The farm is known for its commitment to sustainability and organic farming practices.

6. Kona Joe Coffee:

•   Location: Located just south of Kailua-Kona, Kona Joe Coffee offers guided tours of their coffee plantation.

•   Highlights: Explore the trellised coffee trees and learn about their patented "trellising" method. Enjoy a coffee tasting with ocean views.

•   Additional Info: The location is known for its picturesque views of the Kona coastline.

Visiting these coffee plantations provides a unique opportunity to immerse yourself in the world of Kona coffee, learn about the coffee-growing process, and savor some of the finest coffee in Hawaii. Be sure to check the plantation websites or contact them directly for tour availability and reservations.

Historical Sites in Kona

Kona, Hawaii, is rich in history and culture, offering a variety of historical sites that provide insights into the island's past. Here are some historical sites you should consider visiting in Kona:

1. Pu'uhonua o Honaunau National Historical Park:
  • Description: Also known as the Place of Refuge, this sacred site was a place of sanctuary for ancient Hawaiians who broke kapu (taboos). Explore reconstructed temples, royal grounds, and learn about Hawaiian culture.

2. Hulihe'e Palace:
  • Description: This historic palace in Kailua-Kona was once a vacation home for Hawaiian royalty. It now serves as a museum showcasing Hawaiian artifacts and history.

3. Mokuaikaua Church:

•   Description: Located in Kailua-Kona, Mokuaikaua Church is Hawaii's oldest Christian church. Visit this historic site to learn about its role in the island's history.

4. Kamakahonu National Historic Landmark:

•   Description: This historical landmark in Kailua-Kona was the residence of King Kamehameha I and later served as a residence for Hawaiian monarchs. It's a significant cultural site.

5. Kaloko-Honokohau National Historical Park:

•   Description: Explore this park to discover Hawaiian fishponds, petroglyphs, and historical sites in a beautiful coastal setting.

6. Kealakekua Bay State Historical Park:

•   Description: Visit this site to learn about Captain James Cook's historical landing and explore the Captain Cook Monument, which commemorates his life and achievements.

7. Keauhou Holua Slide:

•   Description: Discover the ancient Hawaiian sport of holua, or lava sledding, at this historical site near Keauhou Bay. The slides are remnants of an ancient sport and cultural tradition.

8. Kahaluu Bay Petroglyphs:
- Description: Located near Kahaluu Beach Park, this site features ancient petroglyphs etched into lava rock, offering a glimpse into the island's indigenous culture.

9. Lapakahi State Historical Park (a bit of a drive from Kona):
- Description: Explore the remains of a traditional Hawaiian fishing village at this historical park on the Kohala Coast. It provides insights into pre-contact Hawaiian life.

10. Pu'ukohola Heiau National Historic Site (a bit of a drive from Kona):
- Description: Visit this massive temple built by King Kamehameha I, known for its historical and cultural significance.

11. Holualoa Village:
- Description: Stroll through this charming village in the hills above Kona, known for its art galleries, historic buildings, and coffee heritage.

These historical sites in Kona offer a deeper understanding of Hawaiian history, culture, and the significance of this beautiful region in shaping Hawaii's past. Make sure to check for any entry fees, hours of operation, and guided tours when planning your visits.

Beaches in Kona, Hawaii

Kona, Hawaii, is known for its beautiful beaches, each offering a unique experience for visitors. Here are some of the top beaches you can explore in the Kona region:

1. Magic Sands Beach (La'aloa Beach Park):
• Description: Also known as Disappearing Sands Beach, it's famous for its white sandy shores that can sometimes vanish due to strong surf. Great for bodyboarding and swimming.

2. Kahaluu Beach Park:
• Description: This is a popular snorkeling spot where you can encounter colorful fish and sea turtles in a protected cove. Facilities include picnic areas and showers.

3. Kua Bay (Manini'owali Beach):
• Description: Known for its stunning white sand and crystal-clear waters, Kua Bay is perfect for swimming and sunbathing. There's limited shade, so be prepared with sunscreen.

4. Hapuna Beach State Recreation Area:
• Description: Located north of Kona, Hapuna Beach is one of the largest and most beautiful white sand beaches on the Big Island. It's great for swimming, sunbathing, and picnicking.

5. Spencer Beach Park:

- Description: A family-friendly beach with calm waters, ideal for swimming and snorkeling. Facilities include restrooms, showers, and picnic areas.

6. Mauna Kea Beach:

- Description: This pristine beach is adjacent to the Mauna Kea Beach Hotel. It's known for its soft, golden sands and excellent swimming conditions.

7. Kealakekua Bay:

- Description: Accessible by boat or a challenging hike, this marine sanctuary offers exceptional snorkeling with an abundance of marine life and coral formations.

8. Pu'uhonua o Honaunau Beach (Two Step):

- Description: Adjacent to the Place of Refuge, this beach is a popular snorkeling and diving location. The "Two Step" entry point makes it easy to access the underwater wonders.

9. Ho'okena Beach Park:

- Description: A black sand beach where you can relax, swim, and enjoy the sun. It's also known for its camping facilities.

10. Makalawena Beach:

• Description: A remote and stunning beach accessible by a hike or four-wheel-drive vehicle. It's a serene spot for sunbathing and picnicking.

11. Anaehoomalu Bay (A-Bay):

• Description: Located within the Waikoloa Beach Resort area, A-Bay offers a sandy shoreline, water sports, and beautiful sunsets.

12. Old Kona Airport Beach Park:

• Description: This beach park offers a unique black sand beach and is ideal for picnics, beachcombing, and watching colorful sunsets.

13. Punalu'u Black Sand Beach (a bit of a drive from Kona):

• Description: Famous for its jet-black sands, this beach is a great place to see sea turtles and explore the unique volcanic landscape.

These beaches in the Kona area offer a wide range of experiences, from snorkeling and swimming to sunbathing and picnicking. Be sure to check the surf and weather conditions before visiting, and practice responsible beach etiquette by respecting the environment and local guidelines.

Outdoor Adventures in Kona, Hawaii

Kona, Hawaii, is a paradise for outdoor adventurers, offering a wide range of exciting activities and experiences in its beautiful natural surroundings. Here are some outdoor adventures to consider when visiting Kona:

1. Snorkeling and Scuba Diving:
•   Description: Explore the vibrant underwater world of Kona's clear waters. Popular snorkeling spots include Kahaluu Beach Park, Kealakekua Bay, and Pu'uhonua o Honaunau.

2. Hiking:
•   Description: Discover scenic trails and hikes throughout the Kona region. Options include the Pu'uhonua o Honaunau National Historical Park coastal trail, Mauna Kea summit hike, and Waipio Valley trails (a bit of a drive from Kona).

3. Ziplining:
•   Description: Experience the thrill of ziplining through lush Hawaiian landscapes. Several ziplining tours are available on the Big Island, including options near Kona.

4. Stand-Up Paddleboarding (SUP):
- Description: Paddleboard along calm bays, rivers, and coastal areas. Rentals and guided tours are readily available.

5. Kayaking:
- Description: Explore the ocean by kayak, with opportunities for guided tours, sea cave exploration, and even kayak fishing.

6. Whale Watching (seasonal, typically December to April):
- Description: Join a whale-watching tour to witness humpback whales during their annual migration to Hawaiian waters.

7. Deep-Sea Fishing:
- Description: Kona is famous for its deep-sea fishing, particularly for marlin. Book a fishing charter for a chance to reel in big catches.

8. Biking:
- Description: Rent a bike and explore the scenic landscapes of Kona, from coastal roads to uphill trails.

9. Horseback Riding:
- Description: Discover the beauty of Kona's landscapes on horseback with guided horseback riding tours.

10. Cave Exploration:
• Description: Explore lava tubes and caves in the Kona region, such as the Kaumana Caves (a bit of a drive from Kona) and Thurston Lava Tube in Hawaii Volcanoes National Park.

11. Sunset Cruises:
• Description: Enjoy a romantic sunset cruise along the Kona coast with opportunities for dolphin and whale watching.

12. Stargazing:
• Description: Visit the Mauna Kea summit for world-class stargazing. Join a guided tour to experience the island's exceptional night skies.

13. ATV Tours:
• Description: Embark on adventurous ATV tours through the rugged terrain of the Big Island, exploring volcanic landscapes and scenic vistas.

14. Parasailing:
• Description: Soar high above the Pacific Ocean while parasailing and enjoy breathtaking views of the coastline.

15. Cultural Tours:

•　　Description: Discover the rich Hawaiian culture through cultural tours, which may include hula and ukulele lessons, lei making, and learning about traditional practices.

Whether you're an adrenaline junkie seeking adventure or prefer a more relaxed outdoor experience, Kona offers a wide array of activities to suit your interests. Be sure to check for tour availability, safety guidelines, and reservations when planning your outdoor adventures in Kona.

Cultural Experiences in Kona, Hawaii

Kona, Hawaii, offers a rich tapestry of cultural experiences that allow you to immerse yourself in the vibrant Hawaiian culture and history. Here are some cultural experiences to consider when visiting Kona:

1. Hula and Ukulele Lessons:

•　　Description: Learn the art of hula dancing and play the sweet sounds of the ukulele with lessons offered by local experts. It's a fun way to connect with Hawaiian traditions.

2. Lei Making Workshops:

•　　Description: Create your own beautiful lei using fresh flowers and learn about the significance of leis in Hawaiian culture. Many resorts and cultural centers offer lei-making classes.

3. Luau:

•   Description: Attend a traditional Hawaiian luau for an evening of music, dance, and delicious Hawaiian cuisine. Luaus are not only entertaining but also educational, showcasing cultural stories and performances.

4. Visit Cultural Centers:

•   Description: Explore cultural centers like the H.N. Greenwell Store Museum, where you can learn about the history of Kona's coffee industry and Hawaiian plantation life.

5. Pu'uhonua o Honaunau National Historical Park:

•   Description: This sacred site, also known as the Place of Refuge, offers a glimpse into ancient Hawaiian culture with reconstructed temples and royal grounds.

6. Kona Coffee Farm Tours:

•   Description: Discover the history and traditions of Kona's coffee industry with guided tours of coffee farms. Learn about the coffee-making process and enjoy tastings.

7. Art Galleries and Studios:

•   Description: Explore the vibrant local art scene in Kona by visiting art galleries and studios. Many local artists draw inspiration from the island's natural beauty and culture.

8. Cultural Festivals:
*   Description: Check if there are any cultural festivals or events happening during your visit. These often feature traditional music, dance, crafts, and cuisine.

9. Cultural Performances:
*   Description: Attend cultural performances that showcase Hawaiian music, hula, and storytelling. Many resorts and venues host regular performances.

10. Traditional Hawaiian Food:
*   Description: Savor traditional Hawaiian dishes like poi, kalua pig, laulau, and lomi lomi salmon at local restaurants and luaus.

11. Visit Historic Sites:
*   Description: Explore historic sites such as Hulihe'e Palace, Mokuaikaua Church, and the Kamakahonu National Historic Landmark to learn about the island's history and Hawaiian royalty.

12. Cultural Workshops:
*   Description: Participate in workshops where you can create traditional Hawaiian crafts, including weaving, carving, and kapa (bark cloth) making.

13. Learn About Petroglyphs:
•   Description: Visit sites with ancient Hawaiian petroglyphs and gain insights into the island's indigenous culture and art.

14. Traditional Outrigger Canoe Paddling:
•   Description: Experience the art of outrigger canoe paddling, an integral part of Hawaiian culture, with guided tours or lessons.

15. Explore Local Markets:
•   Description: Browse local farmers' markets and craft markets to discover handmade crafts, jewelry, and art while interacting with local artisans.

These cultural experiences offer a deeper appreciation for the rich heritage of Hawaii and the people who call Kona home. Whether you're interested in dance, music, crafts, or simply enjoying traditional Hawaiian flavors, Kona provides ample opportunities to engage with the island's unique culture.

Hawaiian Traditions in Kona, Hawaii

Hawaii is a place steeped in rich cultural traditions, and Kona on the Big Island is no exception. Here are some key Hawaiian traditions that you can experience and learn about in Kona:

1. Aloha Spirit:

• Description: *"Aloha"* is more than just a greeting in Hawaii; it's a way of life. The Aloha Spirit represents a warm and welcoming attitude, love, and respect for others. You'll feel it in the hospitality of Kona's people.

2. Hula Dance:

• Description: Hula is the traditional dance of Hawaii, and it tells stories through graceful movements and gestures. You can watch hula performances at luaus, cultural centers, and events in Kona.

3. Ukulele Music:

• Description: The ukulele is a beloved musical instrument in Hawaii. Listen to the sweet melodies of the ukulele at local performances or even try your hand at playing it.

4. Lei-Giving:

• Description: Giving and receiving leis is a common Hawaiian tradition. These garlands made of flowers, leaves, or shells are given as a sign of affection, respect, or welcome. You can participate in lei-making workshops in Kona.

5. Hawaiian Language:

• Description: The Hawaiian language, though not as widely spoken today, is an important part of the culture.

You can learn some basic Hawaiian phrases and words during your visit.

6. Ohana (Family):

•   Description: Family is central to Hawaiian culture, and the concept of "Ohana" emphasizes the importance of family bonds and community. Respect for elders is a fundamental value.

7. Hawaiian Feast (Laua):

•   Description: Luaus are traditional Hawaiian feasts that showcase Hawaiian cuisine, music, and dance. Experience the flavors of Hawaiian dishes like kalua pig, poi, and lomi lomi salmon at a luau in Kona.

8. Ho'oponopono:

•   Description: This Hawaiian practice of conflict resolution and forgiveness is based on restoring harmony and balance in relationships. While not something you can participate in as a tourist, it reflects Hawaiian values.

9. Respect for Nature:

•   Description: Hawaiians have a deep connection to the land and the sea. It's a tradition to respect and care for the natural environment, including the protection of sacred sites and respecting ocean conservation efforts.

10. Canoe Paddling:

• Description: Traditional Hawaiian outrigger canoe paddling is an important cultural activity. You can watch or even join guided canoe tours in Kona.

11. Pele and Hawaiian Mythology:

• Description: Hawaiian mythology includes stories of gods and goddesses, with Pele, the goddess of volcanoes, being a prominent figure. Learn about these myths and legends through cultural presentations and storytelling.

12. Kapu System (Historical):

• Description: In ancient Hawaii, the kapu system consisted of strict rules and taboos. Learn about the history of the kapu system at places like Pu'uhonua o Honaunau National Historical Park.

13. Awa Ceremony:

• Description: The Awa ceremony involves the consumption of a traditional beverage made from the kava root. While it's not as common as it once was, you can still find cultural presentations and explanations of the ceremony.

14. Pelekane (Royal Court):

• Description: While not a current tradition, you can learn about the Hawaiian monarchy's history and visit historical sites like Hulihe'e Palace and Kamakahonu National Historic Landmark.

15. Celebration of Makahiki (Historical):
•   Description: The Makahiki season was a traditional Hawaiian harvest festival marked by sports, games, and feasting. While it's not widely observed today, you can explore its history through cultural centers.

These traditions provide a window into the heart and soul of Hawaiian culture. Participating in or learning about these customs during your visit to Kona can deepen your appreciation for the island's heritage and the enduring spirit of Hawaii.

Art Galleries in Kona, Hawaii

Kona, Hawaii, is home to a vibrant art scene with numerous galleries and studios that showcase a wide range of artistic expressions. Here are some notable art galleries in Kona:

1. Holualoa Village:
•   Description: Holualoa is known as the "Art District" of Kona. Stroll along Mamalahoa Highway and explore a variety of galleries and studios featuring local art, from paintings and ceramics to jewelry and woodwork.

2. Donkey Mill Art Center:

•   Description: Located in Holualoa, this center promotes contemporary art through exhibitions, workshops, and community events. It's a hub for artistic creativity on the Big Island.

3. Ipu Arts Plus Gallery:

•   Description: Situated in Holualoa, this gallery specializes in traditional and contemporary Hawaiian art, including paintings, sculptures, ceramics, and more.

4. Holualoa Gallery:

•   Description: This gallery in Holualoa features a diverse collection of fine art, including paintings, glasswork, jewelry, and sculptures, created by local and international artists.

5. Lewi Gallery:

•   Description: Another gem in Holualoa, Lewi Gallery showcases a wide range of art, from vibrant paintings to unique jewelry and glass art.

6. Studio 7 Gallery:

•   Description: Located in Kailua-Kona, this gallery offers a mix of contemporary art and traditional Hawaiian crafts, including paintings, sculptures, and jewelry.

7. Kona Oceanfront Gallery:

• Description: Situated in Kailua-Kona, this gallery specializes in ocean-inspired art, featuring marine life, coastal scenes, and underwater wonders through various mediums.

8. Surfing Art by Felt:

• Description: Discover surf-inspired art at this gallery in Kailua-Kona, with a unique collection of surfboard paintings and memorabilia.

9. Wyland Galleries:

• Description: Founded by renowned marine life artist Wyland, this gallery in Waikoloa offers a stunning collection of marine and ocean-themed art.

10. Gallery of Great Things:

• Description: Located in Kailua-Kona, this gallery showcases a wide array of Hawaiian artwork, jewelry, and crafts crafted by local artists and artisans.

11. Isaacs Art Center (a bit of a drive from Kona):

• Description: Situated in Waimea, this art center features a permanent collection of Hawaiian art, historic artifacts, and rotating exhibitions.

12. Parker Ranch Fine Art (a bit of a drive from Kona):

• Description: Located in Waimea, this gallery offers a selection of fine art, including paintings, sculptures, and photography, often reflecting the beauty of the Big Island.

13. Hale Halawai Artisans Fair (seasonal events):

• Description: Keep an eye out for seasonal Hale Halawai Artisans Fairs in Kailua-Kona, where local artists showcase their work, including jewelry, textiles, and pottery.

14. Ali'i Drive Artwalk (occasional events):

• Description: Ali'i Drive in Kailua-Kona occasionally hosts artwalk events, providing opportunities to explore pop-up art exhibitions featuring local artists.

15. Gallery of Hawaii Artisans:

• Description: This gallery in Kailua-Kona specializes in showcasing the work of Hawaiian artisans, including handcrafted jewelry, woodwork, ceramics, and more.

These art galleries in Kona offer a diverse and vibrant artistic experience, allowing you to explore the creativity of local and international artists. Whether you're interested in traditional Hawaiian art or contemporary expressions, you'll find a wide range of artistic treasures to admire and purchase.

Chapter 4: Dining in Kona, Hawaii

Kona, Hawaii, offers a delightful dining scene with a mix of traditional Hawaiian cuisine, fresh seafood, and international flavors. Here are some dining options and types of cuisine you can explore in Kona:

Kona's Culinary Scene

Kona's culinary scene is a delightful fusion of traditional Hawaiian flavors, fresh seafood, and international influences. Here's a closer look at what makes Kona's culinary scene unique:

1. Traditional Hawaiian Flavors:
- Description: Kona celebrates its Hawaiian heritage with dishes like kalua pig (smoked and shredded pork), lomi lomi salmon (a salmon salad), and poi (a starchy taro root dish). These traditional flavors can be savored at local restaurants and luaus.

2. Fresh Seafood:
- Description: Thanks to its coastal location, Kona is a seafood lover's paradise. Enjoy mouthwatering dishes like poke (raw fish salad), grilled fish, and seafood platters prepared with locally caught seafood.

3. Kona Coffee:
•   Description: Kona is renowned for its exceptional coffee. Cafes and restaurants proudly serve Kona coffee, and some even offer tours of local coffee farms, providing insight into the coffee-making process.

4. Farm-to-Table Dining:
•   Description: Many Kona restaurants embrace the farm-to-table concept, offering menus that highlight locally sourced ingredients, including fresh produce, meats, and dairy.

5. Asian Fusion:
•   Description: Kona's culinary diversity includes Asian fusion cuisine, where you can savor dishes such as sushi, ramen, and teriyaki with a unique Hawaiian twist.

6. International Flavors:
•   Description: International cuisine abounds in Kona, with restaurants offering Italian, Mexican, Thai, Indian, and more. This variety allows visitors to explore global flavors while in paradise.

7. Food Trucks:
•   Description: Food trucks are a popular dining option in Kona, offering an array of creative and delicious dishes, from gourmet burgers to tacos and more.

8. Luaus:

•   Description: To experience Hawaiian culture and cuisine, attend a traditional luau where you can feast on roasted pig, poi, and tropical desserts while enjoying music and dance.

9. Fine Dining with Ocean Views:

•   Description: Treat yourself to upscale dining with stunning oceanfront views. Kona's fine-dining restaurants offer gourmet menus featuring locally sourced ingredients.

10. Vegetarian and Vegan Options:

-   Description: Those with dietary preferences will find vegetarian and vegan-friendly restaurants in Kona serving plant-based dishes and innovative alternatives.

11. Craft Beer Scene:

-   Description: Kona's craft beer scene is growing, with local breweries and brewpubs offering a range of unique island-inspired beer styles and flavors.

12. Farmers' Markets and Stalls:

-   Description: Explore local farmers' markets and food stalls for a taste of fresh produce, artisanal goods, and homemade snacks. These markets showcase the island's culinary diversity.

13. Beachside Dining:
- Description: Enjoy the ultimate dining experience with your toes in the sand at beachside restaurants, offering spectacular sunsets along with your meal.

14. Culinary Experiences:
- Description: Dive deeper into Kona's culinary culture with cooking classes, farm tours, and other food-related experiences that allow you to learn and taste the island's unique flavors.

15. Kona Breweries:
- Description: For beer enthusiasts, Kona's breweries offer tastings, tours, and a chance to explore the craft beer scene while enjoying the island's natural beauty.

Kona's culinary scene is a testament to the island's rich culture and diverse heritage. Whether you're seeking traditional Hawaiian dishes, fresh seafood, or international cuisine, Kona offers a wide range of dining options to satisfy every palate. Don't miss the opportunity to indulge in the island's delicious and unique culinary offerings during your visit.

Local Hawaiian Cuisine in Kona

Local Hawaiian cuisine is a delicious blend of flavors influenced by the cultural diversity of the islands.

When dining in Kona, you'll have the chance to savor these traditional Hawaiian dishes:

1. Kalua Pig:
•   Description: Kalua pig is a beloved Hawaiian dish made by slow-cooking a whole pig in an underground imu (earth oven) until it's tender and flavorful. The result is succulent, smoky, and often served shredded.

2. Poi:
•   Description: Poi is a starchy dish made from the root of the taro plant. It's pounded and mixed with water to create a smooth, purple-gray paste. Poi can be eaten on its own or as a side dish.

3. Lomi Lomi Salmon:
•   Description: Lomi lomi salmon is a refreshing salad made with diced salmon, tomatoes, onions, and seasonings. It's typically served as a side dish and is known for its bright and tangy flavors.

4. Laulau:
•   Description: Laulau is a traditional Hawaiian dish made by wrapping pork, fish, or chicken with taro leaves and then steaming or baking it until tender. It's a flavorful and savory treat.

5. Hawaiian Plate Lunch:
• Description: A Hawaiian plate lunch typically includes a protein (such as teriyaki chicken, pork, or fish), two scoops of rice, and macaroni salad. It's a hearty and satisfying meal.

6. Loco Moco:
• Description: Loco moco is a comfort food favorite featuring a bed of white rice topped with a hamburger patty, fried egg, and smothered in rich brown gravy.

7. Haupia:
• Description: Haupia is a sweet coconut milk-based dessert often served in the form of a gelatin-like square. It's a delightful way to end a meal with a touch of tropical sweetness.

8. Huli Huli Chicken:
• Description: Huli huli chicken is a flavorful dish made by marinating chicken in a sweet and savory sauce, then grilling it to perfection. It's often served at local fairs and events.

9. Spam Musubi:
• Description: Spam musubi is a popular Hawaiian snack made by placing a slice of Spam (a canned meat product) on a block of rice, wrapping it with nori (seaweed), and seasoning it with soy sauce.

10. Shave Ice:
-   Description: Hawaiian shave ice is a refreshing treat made by shaving a block of ice and topping it with colorful flavored syrups. It's a popular way to cool down on a hot day.

11. Manapua:
-   Description: Manapua is similar to a Chinese bao bun filled with savory fillings like char siu (barbecued pork) or sweet fillings like azuki bean paste.

12. Poke:
-   Description: Poke is a raw fish salad typically made with cubed, marinated fish, often seasoned with soy sauce, sesame oil, seaweed, and other flavorful ingredients.

13. Luau Favorites:
-   Description: At traditional Hawaiian luaus, you can enjoy a feast of these local dishes and more, all while being entertained by hula dancers and live music.

14. Taro and Sweet Potato:
-   Description: Taro and sweet potato are staples in Hawaiian cuisine and can be prepared in various ways, from steamed to fried, showcasing their earthy flavors.

15. Coconut Products:

-   Description: Coconuts are used in numerous dishes, from coconut milk and coconut cream in curries to coconut flakes in desserts and coconut water for refreshment.

Exploring local Hawaiian cuisine in Kona is not just a culinary adventure but also a journey into the rich cultural heritage of the islands. Be sure to try these authentic dishes to experience the true flavors of Hawaii.

Fine Dining in Kona

Kona offers a range of fine dining options, often with stunning oceanfront settings, where you can enjoy a luxurious and memorable culinary experience. Here are some fine dining establishments in Kona:

1. Huggo's:

•   Description: Huggo's is an iconic oceanfront restaurant known for its seafood, steak, and tropical cocktails. It offers a romantic setting with tables right at the water's edge.

2. 'Ulu Ocean Grill:

•   Description: Located at the Four Seasons Resort Hualalai, 'Ulu Ocean Grill specializes in sustainable and locally sourced Hawaiian cuisine, with a focus on fresh seafood and farm-to-table ingredients.

3. Brown's Beach House:
*   Description: Situated at The Fairmont Orchid, Brown's Beach House offers an upscale dining experience with a menu featuring contemporary Hawaiian cuisine, including fresh seafood and island-inspired dishes.

4. CanoeHouse:
*   Description: Found at Mauna Lani Auberge Resorts Collection, CanoeHouse offers panoramic ocean views and a menu showcasing Hawaiian regional cuisine with a modern twist.

5. Roy's Waikoloa Bar & Grill:
*   Description: Roy's is a renowned Hawaiian fusion restaurant with a creative menu that combines Asian and European flavors with a Hawaiian touch. The Waikoloa location is a favorite among visitors.

6. Merriman's:
*   Description: Merriman's in Waimea is known for its commitment to local sourcing and sustainability. The menu features seasonal ingredients from nearby farms and the restaurant's own garden.

7. Napua at Mauna Lani Beach Club:
*   Description: Napua offers oceanfront dining with a focus on fresh seafood, Hawaiian-inspired dishes, and a diverse wine list. It's a perfect spot to enjoy a sunset meal.

8. Manta & Pavilion Wine Bar:

• Description: Located at the Mauna Kea Beach Hotel, Manta & Pavilion Wine Bar offers upscale dining with a focus on Pacific Rim cuisine. Enjoy stunning views and live manta ray viewing in the evenings.

9. Monstera Noodles & Sushi:

• Description: For those seeking Japanese cuisine, Monstera offers a fine dining experience with a menu featuring sushi, sashimi, and delicious noodle dishes in a contemporary setting.

10. Sam Choy's Kai Lanai:

- Description: Sam Choy's Kai Lanai serves Hawaiian regional cuisine with an emphasis on fresh seafood and island flavors. It's known for its welcoming atmosphere and beautiful views.

11. Mediterranean Gourmet:

- Description: Mediterranean Gourmet offers a unique culinary experience with a menu influenced by Mediterranean flavors, featuring dishes like lamb chops, seafood paella, and tapas.

12. Moon and Turtle:

- Description: Located in downtown Hilo (a bit of a drive from Kona), Moon and Turtle is a renowned farm-to-table restaurant known for its creative and seasonal dishes.

13. Café Pesto:

- Description: Also in Hilo, Café Pesto offers an upscale dining experience with a focus on Italian and Pacific Rim cuisine, including fresh seafood and wood-fired pizzas.

14. Sansei Seafood Restaurant & Sushi Bar:

- Description: Located at Queens' MarketPlace in Waikoloa, Sansei is a popular choice for sushi lovers seeking a fine dining experience with a diverse sushi and seafood menu.

15. Tommy Bahama Restaurant & Bar:

- Description: Tommy Bahama offers a relaxed yet elegant dining experience with a menu that combines Caribbean and Pacific Rim flavors, along with an impressive cocktail selection.

These fine dining options in Kona provide the perfect opportunity to indulge in gourmet cuisine while enjoying the beauty of the Hawaiian coastline and a warm island atmosphere. Be sure to make reservations in advance, especially during peak dining hours and seasons.

Casual Eateries in Kona

Kona offers a variety of casual eateries where you can enjoy delicious meals in a relaxed and comfortable atmosphere. Whether you're looking for a quick bite or a leisurely dining experience, here are some casual eateries in Kona:

1. Big Island Grill:

• Description: Big Island Grill is a local favorite known for its hearty portions of Hawaiian comfort food, including loco moco, teriyaki plates, and fresh fish dishes.

2. Da Poke Shack:

• Description: Da Poke Shack is famous for its mouthwatering poke bowls made from fresh, locally caught fish. It's a great spot for a quick and delicious seafood lunch.

3. Basik Açai Café:

• Description: Basik Açai Café offers healthy and refreshing açai bowls, smoothies, and coffee. It's perfect for a nutritious breakfast or snack.

4. Kona Brewing Company:

• Description: Kona Brewing Company serves up craft beer and a menu of pub-style food with a Hawaiian twist. Try their pizzas, burgers, and beer sampler.

5. Island Lava Java:

• Description: Island Lava Java is a popular coffee shop and casual eatery with a beachside location. They offer breakfast, sandwiches, salads, and fresh coffee.

6. Splasher's Grill:

• Description: Splasher's Grill is known for its seafood, burgers, and tropical drinks. It's a great spot to enjoy a casual meal with oceanfront views.

7. Kona Coast Food Tours:

• Description: If you're looking to explore local flavors, consider taking a food tour with Kona Coast Food Tours. You'll visit a variety of casual eateries to sample Hawaiian dishes.

8. Bongo Ben's Island Café:

• Description: Bongo Ben's is a casual café offering breakfast, lunch, and dinner. Enjoy their pancakes, sandwiches, and live music in a laid-back atmosphere.

9. Kona Inn Restaurant:

• Description: Kona Inn Restaurant offers classic American and Hawaiian dishes in a historic setting overlooking the ocean. It's a great place for breakfast or lunch.

10. Krua Thai Cuisine:

- Description: Craving Thai food? Krua Thai Cuisine in Kona serves up a variety of Thai dishes, including curries, noodles, and stir-fries.

11. Sun Dried Specialties:
- Description: Sun Dried Specialties is known for its delicious beef jerky and dried fruit snacks. It's a perfect stop for tasty on-the-go treats.

12. Los Habaneros:
- Description: Los Habaneros offers Mexican cuisine with a Hawaiian twist. Enjoy tacos, burritos, and flavorful salsas in a relaxed atmosphere.

13. Hayashi's You Make the Roll Sushi:
- Description: Create your own sushi rolls at Hayashi's. It's a fun and customizable dining experience for sushi lovers.

14. Ultimate Burger:
- Description: Ultimate Burger is a casual burger joint serving up a variety of burgers, including creative and traditional options, along with fries and shakes.

15. Tropics Ale House:
- Description: Tropics Ale House offers a laid-back setting with a menu featuring pub-style food, including wings, nachos, and a wide selection of craft beers.

These casual eateries in Kona cater to a range of tastes and preferences, making it easy to enjoy a delicious and relaxed meal while exploring the beauty of Hawaii's Big Island.

Vegetarian and Vegan Options in Kona

Kona offers a variety of vegetarian and vegan-friendly restaurants and eateries, making it easy for those with dietary preferences to enjoy delicious meals. Here are some options for vegetarian and vegan dining in Kona:

1. Basik Açai Café:
• Description: Basik Açai Café offers nutritious and plant-based açai bowls, smoothies, and coffee. It's a great spot for vegans and vegetarians looking for a healthy meal.

2. Under the Bodhi Tree:
• Description: Under the Bodhi Tree is a vegetarian and vegan-friendly restaurant offering a diverse menu of plant-based dishes, including salads, wraps, and Buddha bowls.

3. The Vegan Garden:
• Description: The Vegan Garden is a mobile food truck in Kona offering a variety of vegan dishes, from sandwiches and tacos to creative plant-based specialties.

4. Mai Grille:
• Description: Mai Grille, located at The Westin Hapuna Beach Resort, offers a separate vegan menu with options like vegan sushi rolls and plant-based entrees.

5. Kaya's Store:

•   Description: Kaya's Store in Captain Cook, near Kona, features a vegan and vegetarian menu with a focus on fresh and organic ingredients. Enjoy wraps, smoothies, and more.

6. The Coffee Shack:

•   Description: The Coffee Shack in Captain Cook offers vegetarian and vegan breakfast and lunch options, including veggie wraps and delicious fruit smoothies.

7. Happy Kine Vegan and Veggie Cafe:

•   Description: Happy Kine Vegan and Veggie Cafe is known for its vegan and vegetarian Hawaiian plate lunches, showcasing local flavors without animal products.

8. ChoiceMART:

•   Description: ChoiceMART is a natural food store in Kona where you can find a variety of vegetarian and vegan groceries, snacks, and ready-to-eat items.

9. Waimea Coffee Company (a bit of a drive from Kona):

- Description: Waimea Coffee Company offers a selection of vegan and vegetarian breakfast and lunch options in a cozy cafe setting in Waimea.

10. Los Habaneros:

- Description: Los Habaneros offers Mexican cuisine with vegan options, including vegan burritos, tacos, and nachos.

11. Sun Dried Specialties:

- Description: Sun Dried Specialties offers a range of vegetarian and vegan-friendly snacks, including dried fruits and vegetables, making it a great place for on-the-go options.

12. Veg'n Out (a bit of a drive from Kona):

- Description: Located in Hilo, Veg'n Out is a vegan restaurant with a menu that includes burgers, tacos, bowls, and desserts.

13. Island Lava Java:

- Description: Island Lava Java offers vegetarian and vegan options, including vegan pancakes for breakfast and plant-based dishes throughout the day.

14. Tropics Ale House:

- Description: Tropics Ale House has vegan-friendly options, including salads and plant-based appetizers, making it a good choice for those seeking a variety of options.

15. Kona Coast Food Tours:

- Description: Consider taking a food tour with Kona Coast Food Tours, as some tours include stops at eateries with vegetarian and vegan offerings.

These options showcase the growing availability of vegetarian and vegan dining in Kona, allowing visitors to enjoy plant-based meals while exploring the island's culinary scene. Be sure to check with individual restaurants for their current menus and offerings.

Nightlife and Bars in Kona

Kona offers a lively nightlife scene with a mix of bars, lounges, and entertainment options. Whether you're looking for a relaxed evening with a tropical cocktail or a night of dancing and live music, here are some places to explore for nightlife in Kona:

1. Huggo's On The Rocks:
• Description: Huggo's On The Rocks is a popular oceanfront bar known for its tropical drinks, live music, and sunset views. It's a great spot to unwind by the water.

2. Don's Mai Tai Bar:
• Description: Located at the Royal Kona Resort, Don's Mai Tai Bar is a classic tiki bar offering a variety of exotic cocktails and live music in a casual setting.

3. Kona Brewing Company:
• Description: Kona Brewing Company not only serves craft beer but also has a brewpub with a lively atmosphere. Enjoy local beers and pub-style food.

4. Gertrude's Jazz Bar:

• Description: Gertrude's Jazz Bar is known for its live jazz performances, craft cocktails, and cozy ambiance. It's a great place for music enthusiasts.

5. Mai Tai Lounge:

• Description: Located at the Courtyard by Marriott King Kamehameha's Kona Beach Hotel, Mai Tai Lounge offers a variety of tropical drinks and often features live music.

6. Splashers Grill:

• Description: Splashers Grill is not only a great spot for casual dining but also offers a selection of tropical cocktails and drinks with oceanfront views.

7. Kava Kafe:

• Description: If you're interested in trying kava, a traditional Polynesian drink, Kava Kafe offers a unique experience. It's a relaxing spot for a low-key evening.

8. Sushi Shiono:

• Description: Sushi Shiono is known for its sushi and Japanese cuisine but also offers a sake and wine bar where you can enjoy drinks and small bites.

9. The Blue Dragon Restaurant and Musiquarium (a bit of a drive from Kona):

- Description: The Blue Dragon is a unique venue that combines a restaurant, bar, and live music venue. It's known for its eclectic music performances and oceanfront setting.

10. Foster's Kitchen:

- Description: Foster's Kitchen offers craft cocktails and a variety of drinks along with a menu of gourmet cuisine. It's a great place for a night out.

11. Quinn's Almost By the Sea:

- Description: Quinn's offers a relaxed atmosphere with a selection of beer, wine, and cocktails. It's known for its friendly vibe and sunset views.

12. Humpy's Big Island Alehouse:

- Description: Humpy's is a popular sports bar with a wide selection of beers on tap, along with pub grub and often hosts live music events.

13. Daylight Mind Coffee Company:

- Description: Daylight Mind Coffee Company offers a coffeehouse experience during the day and transforms into a wine and cocktail bar in the evenings.

14. Laverne's Sports Bar:

- Description: Laverne's is a sports bar with a laid-back atmosphere, ideal for watching games, enjoying drinks, and playing pool.

15. The Saloon Bar:

- Description: The Saloon Bar offers a dive bar atmosphere with pool tables, dartboards, and a selection of drinks. It's a fun spot for a casual night out.

Please note that the nightlife scene in Kona can vary depending on the day of the week and the time of year, so it's a good idea to check the specific events and entertainment schedules for the time of your visit. Enjoy your evenings exploring Kona's vibrant nightlife!

Chapter 5: Shopping in Kona

Kona offers a variety of shopping experiences, from boutique stores to open-air markets, where you can find unique souvenirs, local crafts, clothing, and more. Here are some places to explore for shopping in Kona:

Souvenirs and Gifts in Kona

When it comes to finding souvenirs and gifts in Kona, you have a wide range of options to choose from. Whether you're looking for traditional Hawaiian mementos, locally made crafts, or unique items that capture the spirit of the Big Island, here are some ideas for souvenirs and gifts:

1. Hawaiian Apparel:
• Description: Look for Hawaiian clothing and accessories, such as aloha shirts, dresses, sarongs, and hats. These make for stylish and comfortable souvenirs.

2. Lei and Fresh Flowers:
• Description: Purchase a lei made from fresh flowers, orchids, or ti leaves. Leis are a symbol of Hawaii and a lovely gift or keepsake.

3. Kona Coffee:
- Description: Kona is famous for its coffee, so consider bringing back a bag of locally grown Kona coffee beans or a selection of coffee-related gifts.

4. Macadamia Nuts:
- Description: Macadamia nuts are a popular Hawaiian snack. You can find them in various flavors, from roasted and salted to chocolate-covered varieties.

5. Hawaiian Jewelry:
- Description: Hawaiian jewelry often features traditional symbols and designs. Look for pieces made from materials like koa wood, pearls, or black coral.

6. Tropical Fruit Preserves:
- Description: Bring home jars of delicious tropical fruit preserves, such as lilikoi (passion fruit) or mango, as a sweet reminder of your trip.

7. Hawaiian Art:
- Description: Explore local art galleries for paintings, sculptures, and other forms of artwork created by Hawaiian artists. These pieces make meaningful gifts.

8. Ukulele:

• Description: Consider buying a ukulele, a traditional Hawaiian musical instrument, as a gift for music enthusiasts or as a unique keepsake.

9. Hawaiian Quilts:

- Description: Hawaiian quilts are known for their intricate patterns and vibrant colors. You can find handcrafted quilts or quilted products like table runners and wall hangings.

10. Handmade Crafts:

- Description: Look for handmade crafts like wooden bowls, carved tiki figures, and woven baskets, which showcase the craftsmanship of local artisans.

11. Surf Gear and Accessories:

- Description: For the surf enthusiasts, you can find surf-related items like board shorts, rash guards, and accessories in Kona's shops.

12. Local Artisanal Products:

- Description: Explore farmers' markets and specialty stores for locally made products such as honey, soaps, candles, and lotions.

13. Hawaiian Books and Literature:

- Description: Discover books about Hawaiian culture, history, or nature, as well as novels by Hawaiian authors for a deeper understanding of the islands.

14. Kukui Nut Leis:

- Description: Kukui nut leis are traditional Hawaiian necklaces. They're often polished and decorated, making them a unique and symbolic gift.

15. Tropical-themed Decor:

- Description: Bring a touch of the tropics to your home with decor items like seashell art, beach-themed photo frames, or Hawaiian-themed wall hangings.

Remember to explore local markets, boutiques, and art galleries to find one-of-a-kind souvenirs and gifts that capture the essence of Kona and the Big Island. Additionally, many shops offer shipping services, so you can send your purchases home if you're concerned about space in your luggage. Enjoy your shopping adventures in Kona!

Local Markets in Kona

Exploring local markets is a fantastic way to experience the vibrant culture of Kona and discover unique items crafted by local artisans.

Here are some local markets in Kona where you can find a variety of goods, from fresh produce to handmade crafts:

1. Kona Farmers' Market:

•	Description: The Kona Farmers' Market is one of the most popular markets on the island. It operates on Wednesdays through Sundays, offering a wide array of fresh produce, local foods, handmade crafts, and souvenirs. It's a great place to find unique gifts and sample delicious Hawaiian snacks.

2. Ali'i Gardens Marketplace:

•	Description: Located in the heart of Kona, Ali'i Gardens Marketplace features local vendors selling handmade jewelry, clothing, art, and more. It's a charming open-air market with a variety of artisanal products.

3. Keauhou Farmers' Market:

•	Description: The Keauhou Farmers' Market, held every Saturday, offers fresh produce, baked goods, prepared foods, and artisan crafts. It's a relaxed market with a lovely oceanfront location.

4. Pure Kona Green Market:

•	Description: This farmers' market is dedicated to organic and sustainably grown produce and products. It's a place to find healthy, eco-friendly options while supporting local farmers.

5. South Kona Green Market:

- Description: The South Kona Green Market operates on Sundays and focuses on local crafts, jewelry, art, and unique gifts. It's a community-oriented market with a friendly atmosphere.

6. Holualoa Village Farmers and Artists Market:

- Description: Located in the charming village of Holualoa, this market showcases local artists and farmers. You can browse pottery, paintings, jewelry, and fresh produce while enjoying a laid-back atmosphere.

7. Waimea Town Market at Parker School (a bit of a drive from Kona):

- Description: Held on Saturdays, this market in Waimea offers a mix of fresh produce, artisanal products, and ready-to-eat foods. It's a great stop if you're exploring the northern part of the island.

8. Waikoloa Village Farmers Market (a bit of a drive from Kona):

- Description: This market, held on Wednesdays and Saturdays, features local vendors selling fresh produce, baked goods, crafts, and more. It's situated in the Waikoloa Village shopping center.

9. Kailua Village Artists' Gallery and Gift Shop:
   - Description: This gallery and gift shop in Kailua Village showcases the work of local artists, including paintings, photography, jewelry, and other handmade items.

10. Kona Commons Farmers' Market:
   - Description: Held every Sunday in the Kona Commons shopping center, this market offers fresh produce, food vendors, and artisanal products in a convenient location.

Visiting these local markets allows you to connect with the community, support local businesses, and find unique treasures that capture the essence of Kona and the Big Island. Each market has its own character and offerings, so take your time exploring them during your stay.

Art and Crafts in Kona

Kona is a haven for art and crafts enthusiasts, with a thriving community of local artisans and galleries that showcase their work. Whether you're interested in paintings, ceramics, textiles, or other forms of art, here are some places to explore in Kona for art and crafts:

1. Holualoa Village:
   • Description: Holualoa Village is known for its artistic community and numerous galleries.

Stroll through the village to discover a wide range of art, including paintings, sculptures, and ceramics. You can often meet the artists and learn about their creative processes.

2. Kona Coffee Living History Farm:
•   Description: This historical farm offers insights into the history of Kona coffee. You can explore the farm's gift shop, where you'll find coffee-related gifts and local art.

3. Holualoa Gallery:
•   Description: Holualoa Gallery is a prominent art space in the village, showcasing a diverse selection of paintings, sculptures, and other artworks created by local and Hawaiian artists.

4. Donkey Mill Art Center:
•   Description: The Donkey Mill Art Center is a hub for creativity, offering art classes, exhibitions, and workshops. It's a great place to see and purchase art from both emerging and established artists.

5. High Fire Hawaii:
•   Description: High Fire Hawaii is a pottery studio and gallery in Holualoa. Explore their collection of handcrafted ceramics and pottery, including functional and decorative pieces.

6. Ali'i Drive Art Walk:

•   Description: Ali'i Drive in Kona often hosts art walks, where local artists display their work along the street. It's an excellent opportunity to discover a variety of art and meet the creators.

7. Hualalai Art and Music Festival:

•   Description: If your visit coincides with the Hualalai Art and Music Festival, don't miss it. This annual event features local art, live music, and cultural performances.

8. Art Galleries at Mauna Lani (a bit of a drive from Kona):

•   Description: The Mauna Lani resort area features several art galleries that display Hawaiian and international art. It's a great place to find unique pieces in an upscale setting.

9. Hawaiian Quilt Collection:

- Description: Hawaiian Quilt Collection offers beautiful handcrafted Hawaiian quilts and quilted products, showcasing the intricate artistry of quilt-making.

10. Local Craft Fairs and Farmers' Markets:

- Description: Keep an eye out for craft fairs and farmers' markets where local artisans often sell their handmade crafts, including jewelry, textiles, and more.

11. Kona Village Artisans:

- Description: Kona Village Artisans is a cooperative gallery featuring the work of local artists and crafters. It's a wonderful place to find unique gifts and support the local creative community.

12. Kona Coast Fine Art:

- Description: This art gallery in Kailua-Kona offers a selection of contemporary art, including paintings, sculptures, and glasswork, created by both local and international artists.

13. Kona Coffee Cultural Festival (seasonal):

- Description: If you visit during the Kona Coffee Cultural Festival, you can explore local art exhibits along with celebrating the rich heritage of Kona coffee.

14. Keauhou Shopping Center:

- Description: Keauhou Shopping Center often hosts art events and exhibits, making it a good place to discover local art while shopping for other items.

15. Art Studios and Workshops:

- Description: Some local artists offer workshops or studio visits where you can see their creative process and even create your own art.

Exploring Kona's art scene provides a deeper understanding of the local culture and allows you to take home a piece of the island's creative spirit. Whether you're a collector or simply appreciate art, you'll find plenty to admire and enjoy in Kona.

Specialty Shops in Kona

Kona boasts a variety of specialty shops that cater to a wide range of interests and preferences. These shops offer unique products and experiences, making them excellent places to explore during your visit. Here are some specialty shops in Kona worth checking out:

1. Kona Natural Soap Company:

• Description: This shop specializes in handmade soaps and skincare products crafted with natural ingredients. You can find a variety of fragrances and skincare items, making it an excellent spot for gifts or personal indulgence.

2. The Original Donkey Balls Factory and Store:

• Description: The Original Donkey Balls Factory is known for its delicious chocolate and macadamia nut treats. Visit the store to sample and purchase these local delicacies.

3. Peaberry and Galette:
• Description: Peaberry and Galette is a specialty coffee shop offering a selection of gourmet coffees and freshly baked pastries. It's perfect for coffee lovers looking for unique blends.

4. The Spoon Shop:
• Description: The Spoon Shop is a unique store specializing in hand-carved wooden spoons, bowls, and other kitchen items. Each piece is a work of art and a functional utensil.

5. The Perfect Gift:
• Description: As the name suggests, this shop is an ideal place to find gifts and souvenirs. They offer a diverse range of products, from home decor to jewelry, many of which are locally made.

6. Hawaii Pacific Parks Association:
• Description: Located within the national park visitor center, this shop offers books, maps, and educational materials related to Hawaii's national parks. It's a great place to learn about the natural and cultural heritage of the islands.

7. Green Flash Coffee:
• Description: Green Flash Coffee specializes in freshly roasted Kona coffee beans. You can purchase bags of coffee to take home or enjoy a cup at their cafe.

8. Kona Abalone:

- • Description: Kona Abalone offers abalone shells and abalone-related products. It's a unique shop to explore Hawaiian marine life and find beautiful shells for decorative purposes.

9. Pacific Fine Art:

- Description: Pacific Fine Art is an art gallery specializing in contemporary and traditional Hawaiian art. It's a place to view and purchase paintings, sculptures, and more from local artists.

10. Hawaii Craftsmen:

- Description: Hawaii Craftsmen is an artisan cooperative offering a variety of handcrafted items, including pottery, jewelry, textiles, and woodwork. It's a great place to discover unique gifts.

11. Mokulele Farms:

- Description: Mokulele Farms specializes in producing gourmet Hawaiian vanilla products. You can find vanilla beans, extract, and other vanilla-infused goods.

12. 808 Clothing:

- Description: 808 Clothing offers a selection of stylish and comfortable Hawaiian-themed apparel. It's a great shop for those looking to bring a piece of Hawaii's fashion culture home.

13. Bead It!:

- Description: Bead It! is a bead store with a wide variety of beads, gemstones, and jewelry-making supplies. It's a creative hub for jewelry enthusiasts.

14. The Quilt Passions:

- Description: If you're interested in quilting, The Quilt Passions offers a selection of fabrics, patterns, and quilting supplies. It's a haven for quilting enthusiasts.

15. Blue Ginger Gallery:

- Description: Blue Ginger Gallery showcases Hawaiian art, jewelry, and crafts with a focus on ocean-inspired themes. It's a great place to find coastal and marine-themed decor.

These specialty shops in Kona cater to diverse interests, whether you're a coffee connoisseur, a lover of artisanal products, or someone seeking unique gifts and souvenirs. Take your time exploring these stores to discover hidden gems and local treasures.

Chapter 6: Practical Information for Your Trip to Kona

To help you plan your trip to Kona effectively, here's some practical information that covers various aspects of your visit, including weather, transportation, currency, and more:

1. Weather:

• Description: Kona generally enjoys a sunny and warm climate. However, keep in mind that weather can vary, so it's advisable to check the forecast before your trip. Pack sunscreen, sunglasses, and lightweight clothing for daytime activities, and bring a light jacket or sweater for cooler evenings.

2. Transportation:

• Description: Kona International Airport (KOA) is the main airport serving the area. From the airport, you can rent a car, take a shuttle, or use ridesharing services to get to your accommodation. Public transportation options are limited, so a rental car is recommended if you plan to explore the island.

3. Currency:

• Description: The currency used in Kona is the United States Dollar (USD).

Credit and debit cards are widely accepted, but it's a good idea to carry some cash for small purchases and places that may not accept cards.

4. Language:

• Description: English is the official language in Hawaii, and it's widely spoken. You'll have no trouble communicating in English during your visit.

5. Time Zone:

• Description: Kona is in the Hawaii-Aleutian Standard Time Zone (HST), which is 10 hours behind Coordinated Universal Time (UTC-10:00). Hawaii does not observe Daylight Saving Time, so the time remains consistent throughout the year.

6. Electricity:

• Description: The standard voltage in Kona is 120V, and the power plugs and sockets are of type A and B. If your devices use a different type of plug or voltage, consider bringing a suitable adapter or converter.

7. Health and Safety:

• Description: Kona is a generally safe destination for travelers. However, it's a good practice to stay hydrated, use sunscreen, and follow safety guidelines when engaging in outdoor activities. Make sure you have travel insurance to cover unexpected medical expenses.

8. Local Laws and Customs:

• Description: Respect the local culture and environment. Avoid touching or disturbing wildlife, and follow any posted signs and regulations in protected areas. It's also customary to remove your shoes when entering someone's home in Hawaii.

9. Emergency Numbers:

• Description: In case of emergencies, dial 911 for police, medical, or fire assistance. Kona has well-equipped medical facilities and hospitals to address healthcare needs.

10. Tipping:

- Description: Tipping is customary in Kona and throughout Hawaii. It's common to leave a 15-20% tip for servers at restaurants and cafes. Additionally, you may consider tipping tour guides and hotel staff for exceptional service.

11. Wi-Fi and Connectivity:

- Description: Most accommodations, restaurants, and cafes in Kona offer Wi-Fi access. If you need mobile data, you can purchase a SIM card or a prepaid mobile hotspot device upon arrival at the airport or local stores.

12. Travel Documents:

- Description: Ensure you have all necessary travel documents, including your passport, visa (if required), and any travel permits for specific activities or parks. Check the expiration dates well in advance.

13. Time Zone Differences:

- Description: Hawaii does not observe Daylight Saving Time, so the time difference with the mainland U.S. and other regions may vary throughout the year. Keep this in mind when making travel plans or scheduling activities.

14. Sun Protection:

- Description: The sun in Kona can be intense. Don't forget to use sunscreen with a high SPF, wear a hat and sunglasses, and stay hydrated to protect yourself from sunburn and heat-related issues.

15. Respect Local Culture:

- Description: Hawaiians have a rich cultural heritage. Show respect for local customs and traditions. For example, it's considered respectful to ask for permission before entering someone's private property.

Planning ahead and being informed about these practical aspects of your trip will help ensure a smooth and enjoyable visit to Kona, allowing you to make the most of your time on the beautiful Big Island of Hawaii.

Tips for a Sustainable Visit to Kona

Promoting sustainability during your visit to Kona and the Big Island is important to help preserve the natural beauty and cultural heritage of the region. Here are some tips for a sustainable and eco-friendly trip:

1. Support Local Businesses:

• Description: Choose locally owned accommodations, restaurants, and shops to support the local economy and reduce the carbon footprint associated with large chain businesses.

2. Reduce Plastic Use:

• Description: Hawaii has taken steps to reduce plastic waste. Bring a reusable water bottle, shopping bag, and reusable utensils to minimize single-use plastics during your trip.

3. Respect Nature and Wildlife:

• Description: Admire wildlife from a safe distance and avoid touching or feeding animals. Stay on designated paths to protect fragile ecosystems and respect posted regulations in protected areas.

4. Practice Leave No Trace:

• Description: Whether you're hiking, snorkeling, or enjoying other outdoor activities, follow the Leave No Trace principles. Pack out all trash and litter, and avoid disturbing the natural environment.

5. Conserve Water:

• Description: Hawaii has a limited freshwater supply, so use water sparingly. Take shorter showers, turn off taps when not in use, and consider reusing towels and linens at your accommodation.

6. Opt for Eco-Friendly Tours:

• Description: Choose tour operators and activities that prioritize eco-friendly practices, such as responsible whale watching, snorkeling, or hiking tours that educate participants about the local environment.

7. Use Reef-Safe Sunscreen:

• Description: When swimming or snorkeling, use reef-safe sunscreen to protect your skin without harming coral reefs and marine life. Many stores in Kona offer reef-safe sunscreen options.

8. Respect Hawaiian Culture:

• Description: Learn about and respect Hawaiian customs and traditions.

Be mindful of sacred sites and cultural practices. Support cultural events and artisans who preserve Hawaiian heritage.

9. Reduce Energy Consumption:
•   Description: Conserve energy by turning off lights, fans, and air conditioning when you leave your accommodation. Opt for energy-efficient transportation options.

10. Choose Sustainable Souvenirs:
- Description: When shopping for souvenirs, look for products made from sustainable materials or supporting local artisans. Avoid purchasing items made from endangered or protected species.

11. Participate in Beach Cleanups:
- Description: Join or organize beach cleanups during your visit. Many local organizations and communities hold regular clean-up events to keep beaches and coastal areas pristine.

12. Responsible Water Activities:
- Description: If you're into water sports, such as snorkeling or diving, practice responsible underwater etiquette. Avoid touching or damaging coral reefs, and refrain from collecting marine life as souvenirs.

13. Learn About Local Conservation Efforts:

- Description: Take the opportunity to learn about local conservation efforts and consider contributing to or volunteering with organizations working to protect Hawaii's unique environment.

14. Responsible Hiking:

- Description: If you plan to hike, stick to established trails, and avoid creating new paths to protect the fragile ecosystem. Pack out all trash, and consider taking part in guided eco-friendly hikes.

15. Use Public Transportation or Carpool:

- Description: When exploring the island, consider using public transportation, carpooling, or renting a fuel-efficient vehicle to reduce greenhouse gas emissions from solo driving.

By following these sustainable travel tips, you can enjoy your visit to Kona while minimizing your impact on the environment and contributing to the preservation of the natural and cultural wonders of Hawaii.

Chapter 7: Planning Your Trip to Kona

Planning a trip to Kona requires careful consideration of various aspects to ensure a smooth and enjoyable experience. Here's a step-by-step guide to help you plan your trip effectively:

1. Set Your Travel Dates:
•   Description: Determine when you want to visit Kona, taking into account your work or personal schedule, as well as the best time to travel based on weather and activities you want to enjoy.

2. Create a Budget:
•   Description: Establish a travel budget, including accommodation, transportation, activities, dining, and souvenirs. Consider setting aside some extra funds for unexpected expenses.

3. Choose Accommodation:
•   Description: Research and book your accommodation in advance. Options in Kona range from hotels and resorts to vacation rentals and camping. Consider your preferences and budget when selecting a place to stay.

4. Book Flights:

•	Description: Find and book flights to Kona International Airport (KOA). Compare prices, airlines, and flight times to secure the best deal. Book well in advance for lower fares.

5. Plan Activities:

•	Description: Create a list of activities and attractions you want to experience in Kona and the Big Island. Prioritize must-see places and activities to ensure you have time for them.

6. Make Reservations:

•	Description: If your activities require reservations, such as guided tours or popular restaurants, book them in advance to secure your spots, especially during peak tourist seasons.

7. Pack Appropriately:

•	Description: Check the weather forecast for Kona during your travel dates and pack accordingly. Include essentials like clothing, swimwear, comfortable shoes, sun protection, and any specialized gear for activities.

8. Travel Insurance:

•	Description: Consider purchasing travel insurance that covers trip cancellations, medical emergencies, and lost luggage. Review the policy to understand what's covered.

9. Travel Documents:

• Description: Ensure you have a valid passport (if needed), any required visas, and your driver's license (if renting a car). Make copies of important documents and store them separately.

10. Plan Transportation:

- Description: Decide on transportation options for getting around Kona and the island. Renting a car is recommended for flexibility, but you can also use shuttles, taxis, or ridesharing services.

11. Dining Reservations:

- Description: If you have specific restaurants you'd like to dine at, make reservations, especially for popular spots. Consider trying local Hawaiian cuisine during your stay.

12. Prepare an Itinerary:

- Description: Create a detailed itinerary that includes your daily activities, reservations, addresses, and contact information. Share it with someone back home in case of emergencies.

13. Travel Health Precautions:

- Description: Check if you need vaccinations or health precautions before traveling to Hawaii. Pack any necessary medications and a basic first-aid kit.

14. Sustainable Travel:

- Description: Plan to be a responsible traveler. Use eco-friendly products, support local businesses, and follow sustainability guidelines during your trip.

15. Emergency Contacts:

- Description: Save important phone numbers, including local emergency contacts, your country's embassy or consulate, and your accommodation's contact information.

16. Final Check:

- Description: Double-check all reservations, documents, and packing lists a few days before your departure to ensure everything is in order.

17. Enjoy Your Trip:

- Description: Once you arrive in Kona, relax, have fun, and savor the experiences the island has to offer. Be flexible with your plans and allow for spontaneous discoveries.

Planning your trip to Kona with attention to detail will help you make the most of your visit and create lasting memories on the beautiful Big Island of Hawaii. Safe travels!

Best Time to Visit Kona

The best time to visit Kona, located on the west coast of the Big Island of Hawaii, largely depends on your preferences for weather, activities, and crowds. Here's a breakdown of the seasons and their characteristics to help you choose the ideal time for your visit:

1. **Winter (December to February):**
• Weather: Winter in Kona is warm, with daytime temperatures typically ranging from 75°F to 85°F (24°C to 29°C). Nights can be cooler but still pleasant.
• Activities: Winter is a great time for whale watching, as humpback whales migrate to Hawaii's warm waters. It's also an excellent season for surfing on the west coast.
• Crowds: While it's generally less crowded than summer, Kona can still see an influx of tourists during the winter holidays.
2. **Spring (March to May):**
• Weather: Spring brings comfortable temperatures with highs in the upper 70s°F to low 80s°F (25°C to 28°C). It's one of the less humid seasons.
• Activities: Spring is ideal for snorkeling and diving, as waters are clear and calm. You can also enjoy hiking without the intense summer heat.
• Crowds: Spring is typically less crowded compared to the winter months.

3. Summer (June to August):
• Weather: Summer in Kona is hot and dry, with temperatures reaching the upper 80s°F to low 90s°F (30°C to 35°C). It's the sunniest season.
• Activities: Summer is perfect for beach days, water sports, and exploring the island. The ocean is calm and warm for swimming and snorkeling.
• Crowds: Summer is a popular tourist season, so expect more crowds, especially in July and August.

4. Fall (September to November):
• Weather: Fall weather in Kona remains warm and pleasant, with temperatures similar to spring. Rainfall increases slightly compared to summer.
• Activities: Fall is a great time for outdoor adventures like hiking and exploring Kona's natural beauty. It's also a good time for golfing.
• Crowds: Crowds begin to taper off in the fall, making it a quieter and more affordable time to visit.

5. Overall Considerations:
• Whale Watching: If you want to see humpback whales, plan your visit during the winter months.
• Budget: Fall and spring are typically considered shoulder seasons, offering a balance of good weather and fewer crowds.
• Diving and Snorkeling: For the best underwater visibility, consider visiting during the spring or fall.
• Surfing: Summer is prime time for surfing on the west coast, but conditions vary by location and skill level.

In summary, the best time to visit Kona depends on your preferences. Winter offers whale watching, spring and fall offer pleasant weather and fewer crowds, while summer is perfect for beach and water activities. Consider your interests and priorities when choosing the season that suits you best.

Travel Itineraries

Creating a travel itinerary for Kona, Hawaii, allows you to make the most of your visit and experience the diverse attractions and activities the area has to offer. Here are two sample itineraries for a 5-day trip to Kona:

Itinerary 1: Beach and Relaxation

Day 1: Arrival in Kona
- Arrive at Kona International Airport (KOA).
- Check-in at your chosen accommodation.
- Unwind and enjoy a sunset view at a beachfront restaurant.

Day 2: Beach Day
- Spend the morning at Kailua-Kona's popular beaches like Magic Sands Beach or Kahaluu Beach Park for snorkeling.
- In the afternoon, explore the Kona Coffee Living History Farm.
- Dine at a beachside restaurant for a seafood feast.

Day 3: Explore Kona
• Visit the Hulihee Palace, a historic royal residence.
• Stroll along Ali'i Drive, exploring art galleries and local shops.
• Take a sunset cruise or enjoy a luau for a taste of Hawaiian culture.

Day 4: Adventure Day
• Explore Hawaii Volcanoes National Park (approximately 2.5 hours from Kona).
• Hike through lava tubes, view steam vents, and visit the Jaggar Museum.
• Return to Kona in the evening and relax with a beachfront dinner.

Day 5: Water Activities
• Try a morning snorkeling or scuba diving excursion.
• Spend the afternoon stand-up paddleboarding or kayaking.
• Have a farewell dinner at a restaurant with ocean views.

Itinerary 2: Adventure and Exploration
Day 1: Arrival in Kona
• Arrive at Kona International Airport (KOA).
• Check-in at your chosen accommodation.
• Relax and acclimate to the island's pace.

Day 2: Volcano Adventure

• Drive to Hawaii Volcanoes National Park (approximately 2.5 hours).

• Explore the park, including Thurston Lava Tube and Kilauea Caldera.

• Stay overnight near the park or return to Kona.

Day 3: Coffee and Culture

• Visit a Kona coffee farm for a tour and tasting.

• Explore the Pu'uhonua o Honaunau National Historical Park.

• Experience a traditional Hawaiian luau in the evening.

Day 4: Water Adventures

• Embark on a morning snorkeling or scuba diving excursion.

• Enjoy an afternoon of deep-sea fishing.

• Savor fresh seafood for dinner.

Day 5: Outdoor Adventures

• Go hiking in the lush Waipio Valley (a day trip from Kona).

• Visit the Pololu Valley Lookout.

• Return to Kona and celebrate your adventure with a sunset dinner.

These itineraries offer a blend of relaxation, adventure, cultural exploration, and outdoor activities to help you make the most of your 5-day trip to Kona. Feel free to adjust them to your preferences and add specific attractions or activities that interest you the most.

Packing Essentials

Packing for your trip to Kona, Hawaii, requires careful consideration of the tropical climate and the activities you plan to enjoy. Here's a list of essential items to pack:

Clothing:

1. Lightweight Clothing: Pack breathable, moisture-wicking shirts, shorts, and dresses for warm weather.

2. Swimwear: Bring swimsuits and beach cover-ups for beach days and water activities.

3. Sun Protection: Include wide-brimmed hats, sunglasses with UV protection, and sun-protective clothing for sun safety.

4. Rain Jacket: Although Kona is known for its dry climate, a light rain jacket or poncho can come in handy for unexpected showers.

5. Comfortable Shoes: Bring comfortable walking shoes, sandals, and water shoes for various activities.

6. Casual Evening Attire: Kona is relatively casual, but you may want slightly dressier outfits for dining out in the evening.

Outdoor Gear:

7. Snorkeling Gear: If you have your own mask, snorkel, and fins, consider bringing them. Otherwise, you can rent them locally.

8. Hiking Gear: If you plan to hike, pack comfortable hiking shoes, moisture-wicking socks, and a daypack with essentials like water, snacks, and a first-aid kit.

Beach and Water Activities:

9. Beach Towel: A compact, quick-drying beach towel is convenient for beach days.

10. Beach Bag: A tote bag or beach bag to carry your essentials.

Sun Protection:

11. Sunscreen: Pack reef-safe sunscreen with high SPF to protect your skin.

12. Aloe Vera: In case of sunburn, aloe vera gel can provide relief.

Health and First-Aid:

13. Prescription Medications: Bring any necessary prescription medications, along with a copy of your prescription.

14. Basic First-Aid Kit: Include bandages, antiseptic wipes, pain relievers, and any personal medications.

Electronics:

15. Travel Adapter: If you're coming from outside the U.S., bring a travel adapter for your electronic devices.

16. Chargers: Don't forget chargers for your phone, camera, and other electronic devices.

Travel Documents and Essentials:

17. Passport and ID: Ensure your passport is valid for at least six months beyond your travel dates.

18. Travel Insurance: Have copies of your travel insurance policy and contact information.

19. Flight Tickets: Digital or printed copies of your flight itineraries.

20. Accommodation Information: Keep confirmation emails and contact information for your accommodations.

Miscellaneous:

21. Reusable Water Bottle: Stay hydrated with a reusable water bottle.

22. Backpack or Daypack: Useful for day trips and carrying essentials.

23. Cash: While credit cards are widely accepted, it's a good idea to carry some cash for small purchases and in case you visit places with limited card acceptance.

24. Travel Guide and Maps: A physical or digital travel guide and maps can be helpful for planning and navigating.

25. Ziplock Bags: Useful for storing snacks, protecting electronics from moisture, or packing wet swimwear.

26. Travel Pillow and Eye Mask: If you're on a long flight or value comfortable sleep.

Remember that Kona has a relaxed atmosphere, so pack light and focus on comfort and sun protection. Be mindful of airline baggage weight limits to avoid excess fees, and consider laundry facilities at your accommodation if you plan to travel light and rewear clothing items.

Traveling with Kids

Traveling to Kona with kids can be a wonderful experience, but it requires some extra planning to ensure a smooth and enjoyable trip for the entire family. Here are some tips for traveling with kids to Kona:

1. **Choose Family-Friendly Accommodation:**
•   Look for accommodations that cater to families. Consider renting a vacation home or condo with kitchen facilities to make meals and snacks more convenient.
2. **Pack Essentials for Kids:**
•   Pack essentials like baby food, diapers, wipes, and any special comfort items your child may need. These items can be more expensive or harder to find on the island.
3. **Plan Kid-Friendly Activities:**
•   Research and plan activities that are suitable for children. Kona offers opportunities for family-friendly snorkeling, beach outings, and exploring nature.

4. Sun Protection:

• Ensure your kids have adequate sun protection, including sunscreen, hats, sunglasses, and UV-blocking swimwear. Reapply sunscreen regularly.

5. Stay Hydrated:

• Keep your kids hydrated, especially in the warm Hawaiian climate. Carry reusable water bottles and refill them regularly.

6. Snacks and Food:

• Pack snacks and small meals for your kids, as well as some familiar foods they enjoy. While Hawaiian cuisine is delicious, having familiar options can be helpful.

7. Plan Rest Time:

• Kids may need breaks and nap times, especially if you're exploring outdoor attractions. Plan rest stops and quiet moments to recharge.

8. Safety First:

• Ensure your child's safety at all times. When near the water, watch them closely, and consider using life jackets if appropriate. Teach them about ocean safety.

9. Child-Friendly Transportation:

• If renting a car, ensure it has appropriate car seats or booster seats for your child's age and size. Familiarize yourself with Hawaii's car seat laws.

10. Entertainment and Distractions:

• Bring entertainment for your kids during travel, such as books, toys, or electronic devices with headphones.

Long flights or drives can be more manageable with distractions.

11. Travel Documents:

• Carry all necessary travel documents for your children, including passports if required. Keep copies in case of loss or emergencies.

12. Involve Kids in Planning:

• Involve your kids in planning some aspects of the trip, like choosing a fun activity or picking a restaurant. This can make them more engaged and excited about the trip.

13. Respect Local Culture:

• Teach your kids about Hawaiian culture and traditions, including respect for the environment and local customs.

14. Health Precautions:

• Be prepared for minor health issues. Pack a small first-aid kit with items like bandages, pain relievers, and antihistamines.

15. Emergency Contacts:

• Keep a list of emergency contacts, including local healthcare facilities and your accommodation's contact information.

16. Be Flexible:

• Be flexible with your itinerary and expectations. Kids may have different needs and interests, so adapt your plans accordingly.

Traveling with kids to Kona can be a memorable and enriching experience for the whole family. With careful planning and consideration for your children's needs, you can create lasting memories in this beautiful Hawaiian destination.

Accessibility

Kona, like many Hawaiian destinations, is generally accessible and welcoming to travelers with varying levels of mobility and accessibility needs. Here are some important considerations and tips for travelers with accessibility requirements:

1. Accessible Accommodations:
• Look for hotels, resorts, or vacation rentals that offer accessible rooms or accommodations with features like wider doorways, grab bars, and roll-in showers.

2. Accessible Transportation:
• Rent an accessible vehicle if needed. Many car rental companies offer accessible vans equipped with ramps and wheelchair restraints.

3. Airport Assistance:
• Notify the airline of any mobility challenges in advance to request assistance at the airport, such as wheelchair service or priority boarding.

4. Accessible Activities:

• Research and inquire about the accessibility of specific activities and attractions in Kona. Some may have wheelchair-friendly paths or accommodations.

5. Beach Accessibility:

• Some beaches in Kona have beach wheelchairs available for rent, and there may be accessible paths or ramps to certain areas.

6. Accessibility Apps and Maps:

• Use accessibility apps and maps that provide information on accessible routes, bathrooms, and facilities.

7. Accessible Tours:

• Look for accessible tours and excursions that cater to travelers with mobility challenges.

8. Communication:

• Communicate your accessibility needs to hotels, restaurants, and tour operators in advance to ensure they can accommodate you.

9. Medical Supplies:

• If you require medical supplies or equipment, bring an adequate supply with you, as specific brands or types may not be readily available.

10. Local Resources:

• Connect with local disability organizations or resources for additional information on accessibility in Kona.

11. Prescriptions and Medications:

• Carry necessary prescriptions and medications, and have a copy of your medical history in case of emergencies.

12. **Emergency Contacts:**
• Keep a list of emergency contacts, including local medical facilities and contact information for your accommodation.

13. **Accessible Restrooms:**
• Be aware of the locations of accessible restrooms, and check if they meet your specific needs.

14. **Respect Local Culture:**
• While in Kona, respect Hawaiian culture and traditions, including the spirit of 'Aloha' (kindness and respect). This applies to everyone, regardless of their accessibility needs.

It's important to note that while Kona has made efforts to improve accessibility, there may still be some limitations, especially in more remote areas. Therefore, thorough research and advance planning are essential to ensure a comfortable and enjoyable visit to Kona for travelers with accessibility requirements.

Useful Hawaiian Phrases

Here are some useful Hawaiian phrases and common English phrases to help you communicate and show respect while in Kona:

1. Aloha - Hello, goodbye, love, and more; the most versatile Hawaiian word.

2. Mahalo - Thank you.
3. A hui hou - Until we meet again.
4. E komo mai - Welcome.
5. 'Ohana - Family.
6. Pau hana - Done with work; it's time to relax.
7. Hale - House.
8. Kai - Ocean.
9. Mauka - Toward the mountains.
10. Makai - Toward the sea.
11. 'Ono - Delicious.
12. Haumāna - Student or learner.
13. Kūpuna - Elder or grandparent.
14. Puka - Hole or opening.
15. Kōkua - Help or assistance.
16. Hana hou - Encore or do it again.
17. Hele - Go or walk.
18. 'Aina - Land or earth.
19. Mālama 'āina - Care for the land; environmental stewardship.

Common English Phrases:

1. Hello!
2. Good morning!
3. Good afternoon!
4. Good evening!
5. How are you?
6. Please.

7. Excuse me.
8. Yes.
9. No.
10. I don't understand.
11. Can you help me?
12. How much does this cost?
13. Where is the restroom?
14. I would like to order…
15. Can I have the check, please?
16. What's your name?
17. My name is…
18. I'm lost.
19. Thank you very much.

Using a few Hawaiian phrases, such as *"Aloha"* and *"Mahalo,"* can go a long way in showing respect for the local culture while English is widely spoken and understood in Kona. Enjoy your trip and your interactions with the warm and welcoming people of Hawaii!

Beyond Kona

Exploring Hawaii Island

While Kona itself offers a wealth of attractions and activities, exploring beyond Kona on the Big Island of Hawaii allows you to discover even more natural beauty, culture, and adventure. Here are some exciting places and experiences to consider beyond Kona:

1. Hawaii Volcanoes National Park: Located approximately 2.5 hours from Kona, this park is home to active volcanoes, lava fields, hiking trails, and the fascinating Thurston Lava Tube. Witness the power of nature as you explore volcanic landscapes.

2. Mauna Kea: Visit the Mauna Kea Observatories for stargazing and enjoy panoramic views from the summit of this dormant volcano. Be prepared for high altitudes and chilly temperatures.

3. Waipio Valley: Known as the "Valley of the Kings," Waipio Valley offers lush greenery, towering cliffs, and a black sand beach. You can hike or take a guided tour into the valley to explore its beauty.

4. Akaka Falls State Park: Witness the stunning Akaka Falls, which plunges 442 feet into a lush gorge. The park features a loop trail with viewpoints of the falls and lush rainforest.

5.   Hilo: The largest town on the Big Island, Hilo offers a taste of Hawaiian history and culture. Visit the Pacific Tsunami Museum, explore the farmers' market, and stroll through the Liliuokalani Gardens.

6.   Punalu'u Black Sand Beach: This unique beach features black sand created by volcanic activity. It's also known for its resident green sea turtles, which you can often spot basking on the shore.

7.   Kohala Coast: Discover the stunning beaches and resorts of the Kohala Coast, home to top-notch golf courses, water activities, and beautiful sunsets.

8.   Pu'uhonua o Honaunau National Historical Park: Explore this ancient Hawaiian place of refuge, where you can learn about Hawaiian history and culture, including sacred temples and a royal palace.

9.   Green Sand Beach (Papakolea Beach): Located near South Point, this unique beach features olive-green sand due to the presence of olivine crystals. A hike is required to reach the beach, or you can take a shuttle.

10.   Captain Cook: Visit the Captain Cook Monument, accessible by hiking, boat tours, or kayaking. This historic site commemorates the arrival of Captain James Cook to the Hawaiian Islands.

11.   Kohala Mountain Road Scenic Drive: Take a scenic drive through the lush and picturesque landscapes of the Kohala Mountain Road, offering stunning views of valleys and waterfalls.

12.   Hawaiian Coffee Farms: Explore the coffee farms in the Kona Coffee Belt and learn about the process of growing and harvesting some of the world's finest coffee beans.

13.   Manta Ray Night Snorkel: Experience the thrill of snorkeling with manta rays at night. Several operators offer guided tours to see these graceful creatures up close.

14.   Paniolo (Hawaiian Cowboy) Culture: Learn about Hawaii's ranching history in Waimea, where you can visit cattle ranches, attend rodeos, and experience the unique Paniolo culture.

Exploring beyond Kona allows you to delve deeper into the diversity of landscapes and experiences that the Big Island of Hawaii has to offer. Whether you're interested in natural wonders, cultural heritage, or outdoor adventures, there's something for everyone to enjoy beyond Kona's shores.

Day Trips and Excursions

Exploring Hawaii Island through day trips and excursions allows you to cover a lot of ground and experience a variety of attractions and activities. Here are some recommended day trips and excursions to consider during your visit to the Big Island:

1. Hilo Day Trip:
•   Start your day early and drive to Hilo on the east coast. Visit the Pacific Tsunami Museum, explore the beautiful Liliuokalani Gardens, and stroll through the Hilo Farmers Market. Don't miss Rainbow Falls and the serene Wailuku River State Park.

2. Waipio Valley Adventure:
•   Take a guided tour or drive to Waipio Valley for a day of adventure. Hike or ride in a 4x4 vehicle to explore this stunning valley, visit the black sand beach, and soak in the lush scenery.

3. Hawaii Tropical Botanical Garden:
•   Combine your visit to Hilo with a trip to the Hawaii Tropical Botanical Garden, where you can explore a paradise of exotic plants and scenic coastal views.

4. Mauna Kea Stargazing Tour:
•   Join an organized stargazing tour to Mauna Kea, which typically includes transportation to the summit, telescopes, and expert guides who provide insights into the night sky.

5. Kohala Waterfall Adventure:
•   Embark on a tour that takes you to Kohala's waterfalls, allowing you to swim in freshwater pools and enjoy the lush landscapes of the island's northwestern region.

6. Kona Coffee Farm Tour:
•   Visit a Kona coffee farm and take a guided tour to learn about the coffee-making process, from bean to cup. Enjoy tastings of freshly roasted coffee.

7.	Captain Cook Snorkeling Cruise:
•	Book a snorkeling cruise to Kealakekua Bay to explore vibrant coral reefs and marine life. Some tours also include a visit to the Captain Cook Monument.

8.	Hawaiian Culture and History Tour:
•	Join a cultural tour that explores historical sites, such as Pu'uhonua o Honaunau National Historical Park, and provides insights into Hawaiian traditions and customs.

9.	Kilauea Helicopter Tour:
•	Experience the Big Island's volcanic landscapes from the air by booking a helicopter tour. You'll witness lava flows, craters, and the breathtaking terrain.

10.	Pololu Valley Adventure:
•	Hike down to Pololu Valley's black sand beach on the northern tip of the island. It offers stunning views and a chance to experience Hawaii's diverse landscapes.

11.	South Point and Green Sand Beach:
•	Take a day trip to South Point, the southernmost point of the United States. Hike to Green Sand Beach and swim in its uniquely colored waters.

12.	Manta Ray Night Dive or Snorkel:
•	For an unforgettable evening adventure, sign up for a manta ray night dive or snorkel experience, offered off the Kona coast.

13.	Paniolo (Hawaiian Cowboy) Tour:
•	Dive into Hawaii's ranching history with a visit to a working cattle ranch, where you can learn about Paniolo culture and enjoy a scenic horseback ride.

14. Kohala Zipline Adventure:
* If you're seeking thrills, consider a zipline adventure in Kohala, where you can soar over lush landscapes and take in panoramic views.

15. Kayaking Adventures:
* Explore the island's coastlines and rivers on a guided kayak tour, which may include opportunities for snorkeling or visiting secluded beaches.

16. Local Food Tours:
* Join a food tour in Kona or Hilo to sample a variety of local dishes, including fresh seafood, tropical fruits, and Hawaiian specialties.

Remember to book tours and excursions in advance, especially during peak tourist seasons. Each of these day trips and excursions offers a unique perspective on Hawaii Island, allowing you to experience its rich natural beauty, culture, and adventure.

Conclusion

In conclusion, exploring Hawaii Island, also known as the Big Island, offers a wealth of natural wonders, cultural experiences, and outdoor adventures. Whether you're witnessing the raw power of volcanoes in Hawaii Volcanoes National Park, stargazing atop Mauna Kea, or enjoying the lush landscapes of Waipio Valley, the Big Island has something for every traveler.

You can embark on day trips to Hilo, Waipio Valley, or the Kohala Coast, each offering its own unique charm. Discover Hawaiian culture and history at places like Pu'uhonua o Honaunau National Historical Park or immerse yourself in the world of coffee on a Kona coffee farm tour.

For those seeking adventure, there are opportunities for snorkeling, ziplining, horseback riding, and much more. And don't forget to indulge in the island's culinary delights, from fresh seafood to traditional Hawaiian dishes.

As you explore this diverse and captivating island, remember to practice sustainable tourism, respect local customs, and immerse yourself in the spirit of 'Aloha.' Hawaii Island promises a memorable and enriching travel experience for all who visit.

Farewell to Kona

Farewell to Kona! I hope you've had an incredible time exploring this beautiful Hawaiian destination. If you ever have more questions or need travel advice in the future, don't hesitate to return. Safe travels, and may your memories of Kona be filled with warmth and aloha spirit!

Further Resources

1. Travel Websites: Websites like TripAdvisor, Lonely Planet, and Fodor's offer in-depth travel guides, reviews, and recommendations for Kona and Hawaii in general.

2. Official Tourism Websites: Check out the official tourism websites for Hawaii and Kona, which often provide up-to-date information on attractions, events, and travel tips.

3. Local Visitor Centers: When in Kona, visit local visitor centers for brochures, maps, and guidance from experts on what to see and do.

4. Travel Blogs: Many travelers share their experiences and insights about Kona on travel blogs. These personal accounts can offer unique perspectives and tips.

5. Social Media: Explore hashtags and accounts related to Kona on platforms like Instagram and Twitter to discover recent photos, posts, and recommendations from other travelers.

6. Travel Forums: Websites like TripAdvisor's forums and Reddit's travel subreddit can be excellent places to ask questions, seek advice, and connect with fellow travelers.

7. Books: Consider reading travel books and guides specific to Hawaii and Kona. Popular titles include "Hawaii: The Big Island Revealed" by Andrew Doughty.

8. Local Events Calendars: Check local event calendars for festivals, cultural events, and activities happening during your visit to Kona.

9. YouTube: Watch travel vlogs and videos about Kona to get visual insights into the destination and discover hidden gems.

10. Travel Apps: Download travel apps like Google Maps, Yelp, and local transportation apps to assist with navigation and finding nearby restaurants and attractions.

Remember that staying informed and planning ahead can enhance your travel experience. Enjoy your future adventures, wherever they may take you!